Breaking the Cycle

New Frontiers in Education
Edited by Dr. Frederick M. Hess

This Rowman & Littlefield Education series provides educational leaders, entrepreneurs, and researchers the opportunity to offer insights that stretch the boundaries of thinking on education. Educational entrepreneurs and leaders have too rarely shared their experiences and insights. Research has too often been characterized by impenetrable jargon. This series aims to foster volumes that can inform, educate, and inspire aspiring reformers and allow them to learn from the trials of some of today's most dynamic doers; provide researchers with a platform for explaining their work in language that allows policymakers and practitioners to take full advantage of its insights; and establish a launch pad for fresh ideas and hard-won experience. Whether an author is a prominent leader in education, a researcher, or an entrepreneur, the key criterion for inclusion in New Frontiers in Education is a willingness to challenge conventional wisdom and pat answers. The series editor, Frederick M. Hess, is the director of education policy studies at the American Enterprise Institute and can be reached at rhess@aei.org or (202) 828-6030.

Breaking the Cycle

How Schools Can Overcome Urban Challenges

Nancy Brown Diggs

ROWMAN & LITTLEFIELD EDUCATION
A division of
ROWMAN & LITTLEFIELD
Lanham • Boulder • New York • Toronto • Plymouth, UK

Published by Rowman & Littlefield Education
A division of Rowman & Littlefield
4501 Forbes Boulevard, Suite 200, Lanham, Maryland 20706
www.rowman.com

10 Thornbury Road, Plymouth PL6 7PP, United Kingdom

British Library Cataloguing in Publication Information Available

Library of Congress Cataloging-in-Publication Data Available

Diggs, Nancy Brown.
Breaking the cycle : how schools can overcome urban challenges / by Nancy Brown Diggs.
p. cm.
Includes bibliographical references and index.
ISBN 978-1-4758-0610-6 (cloth : alk. paper) — ISBN 978-1-4758-0611-3 (paper: alk. paper) — ISBN 978-1-4758-0612-0 (electronic)

♾™ The paper used in this publication meets the minimum requirements of American National Standard for Information Sciences Permanence of Paper for Printed Library Materials, ANSI/NISO Z39.48-1992.

Printed in the United States of America

Contents

Foreword

In the educational deserts of inner-city America, you occasionally find a green tree, a school that successfully equips its students with the knowledge, skills, and other attributes (character, behavior, attitude, aspiration, etc.) that are necessary to succeed in college and adult life.

Many of those terrific schools serve young kids; that is, they are elementary schools—and all too often the girls and boys emerging from them pour into the dreadful high schools that comprise far too much of urban secondary education across this land. Putting it gently, truly effective inner-city high schools are rare. If you limit your search to "open admission" public schools that serve "ordinary" kids, thereby omitting selective-admission, private, and parochial schools, your search is even more challenging. And if you're looking for them in the declining cities of America's "rust belt," places that have lost much of their human and financial capital, their civic energy, their corporate headquarters, and too many of the families with spirit and ambition for themselves and their kids, you're lucky if you find any such schools at all. The odds are too slim, the circumstances too daunting, the kids too afflicted, the budgets too tight, and the leadership too dispirited.

That's why this heartening book by Nancy Brown Diggs is so welcome. It's the tale of a rare exception, an educational green tree that's growing in an environment so adverse that little else by way of public secondary education is thriving.

That's the environment today in my hometown, Dayton, Ohio, once a powerhouse of industry and invention (think of the Wright brothers, Charles F. Kettering, the cash register, General Motors in its heyday, and so much more). Dayton today is plagued by poverty, unemployment, the exodus of major private-sector employers, and the loss of corporate chieftains who once also served as community anchors, leaders, and philanthropists. The city's public-school system displays all the woes of American urban education, as well as shrinking enrollments, failed tax levies, an obdurate teachers union, and (most of the time) a dysfunctional school board that undermines the best efforts of well-meaning superintendents who don't lack for worthy ideas but rarely can find the political backing, financial wherewithal, or administrative support to make them happen. Even Dayton's enormous charter-school sector—now some twenty-seven schools enrolling 6,500 pupils—about one-third of all public-school pupils in the city—has few shining stars. Things just don't grow well in a desert.

But then there's the Dayton Early College Academy (DECA), the remarkable (charter) school that Dr. Diggs profiles in these pages. It's not perfect, but it's working really well—and getting better. It's also growing, its leaders having realized first that they needed to catch these kids before high school and, more recently, that to really have a profound impact they need to start in kindergarten. That's why DECA, which began in August 2003 (as part of the Gates Foundation initiative) as an "early college high school," and added grades 7 and 8 in 2008 and 2009 respectively, has recently been joined by "DECA Prep," a K–6 charter school.

I've intersected with DECA in several ways, besides being a wary watcher who evolved into an enthusiastic booster. The Thomas B. Fordham Foundation, where I work, and which has a longtime interest in Ohio generally and Dayton particularly, is the "authorizer" of DECA Prep. We've made several grants (small by general philanthropic gauges but large for us) to help sustain and grow DECA. Our on-the-ground team in Ohio, especially my long-time colleague Terry Ryan, has played utility infielder for DECA in myriad ways. And the chairman of DECA's board, who also just happens to be married to Dr. Diggs, has long been perhaps our staunchest ally and collaborator on sundry education-reform efforts in the Dayton area.

I cannot begin to do justice to the many other people who in less than a decade have turned DECA from a concept into Dayton's brightest public-education star, but I would be unconscionably remiss if I didn't name former University of Dayton education dean Tom Lasley, who got it going, and DECA superintendent Judy Hennessey, who nurtured it into the tall green tree that it is today.

Tall doesn't mean big. In 2011–2012, DECA enrolled just four hundred kids, all of them there by choice. But it's been remarkably successful at taking kids, most of them black and essentially all poor, from home environments that are often sorely afflicted and prior school experiences that were usually mediocre or worse, and equipping them with the knowledge, skills, and other attributes mentioned above. And the proof—recounted in these pages—is externally validated by the DECA's "excellent with distinction" rating by the Ohio Department of Education and by graduation and college-matriculation rates far higher than any other public secondary school in urban Ohio is producing.

Yes, it's a remarkable school, a star that belongs in America's small constellation of successful "no excuses" charter schools such as KIPP, Achievement First, Harlem Village Academy, YES Prep, Success Academy, and Cleveland's Breakthrough Schools. The others are better known, to be sure, because there are more of them, they're located mainly in major cities, and they've gotten much media attention. But DECA is part of the same constellation.

What's remarkable about this *book*, however, is that it's so much more than the story of an educational institution. Most of it consists of stories of the *people* involved with DECA, above all its students, and much of it is told in their own words. Some of these sagas are heart rending, particularly as kids describe the miserable circumstances of their early lives. But much that's here—very often from the same girls and boys—will uplift your spirit and rekindle your faith in what human beings are capable of becoming—and overcoming—if given a decent chance and access to great schools.

Nancy Diggs has titled it *Breaking the Cycle*, and in truth it recalls "The Little Engine That Could," the beloved children's story of the small locomotive that made it up a very steep hill through grit, hard work, self-confidence, and boundless aspiration. That's what DECA has done already—and will do more and more of in the years to come. It's what American education *could* do in thousands of other places and for millions of other kids. It's what green trees in quantity could do to turn a desert into a healthy forest of successful education and realized human potential.

Chester E. Finn Jr.

Preface

Drugs, violence, crime, fatherless homes—like the Four Horsemen of the Apocalypse, they have galloped in to doom the inner city, each toxic aspect impacting the other. How do you break the vicious cycle? Thanks to a school called DECA, which aspires not only to send all its graduates to college but to keep them there until graduation, there are young people who are doing just that.

Although many Americans of all colors suffer from the culture of poverty, black Americans have borne the additional burdens of a long history of discrimination. Most African Americans, to be sure, are not poor. About half of the black population live solid middle-class lives;[1] more than a third live in the suburbs.[2] And not all families headed by single mothers are dysfunctional. Many unmarried women are strong, dedicated parents who want the best for their children.

Those inner-city residents who merit our attention, however, are those whose statistics point to the challenges their children face: the failure to educate America's children, especially those in the inner cities, is a subject that affects us all and the future of our country, as evidenced by the shocking figures.

While America's students lag well behind other countries in science, reading, and math, the scores of the inner city's African American students are even lower than those of their white peers. The average black twelfth-grader's academic achievement is no higher than the average white eighth-grader's;[3] only 12 percent of black eighth-grade boys are proficient in math, compared to 44 percent of white boys. About half of African American teens graduate from high school—43 percent for males[4]—compared to 76 percent of whites.[5]

While only 12 percent of Americans are black, their numbers make up 44 percent of the prison population, and the homicide rate for black males is seven times that of their white contemporaries.[6]

The cost to the community, both financially and socially, is enormous. By the time they reach their mid-thirties, 60 percent of black, male high school dropouts have been in prison,[7] whereas "fewer than 1 percent of those with bachelor's degrees will be incarcerated."[8] The average cost we bear per inmate is about $25,000 a year,[9] without considering the loss of tax income from which society would benefit if they were employed. With a college degree, on the other hand, a worker can earn over $1 million more than a high-school graduate over a lifetime.[10]

In virtually every inner city in America, young people face a grim future. DECA's hometown, Dayton, Ohio, has been called the quintessential American city, and, as such, it reflects what has been happening throughout the country: the decline of manufacturing jobs that use low-skilled labor, an increase in unemployment, and the high crime rate associated with poverty. Close to one-third of its residents, 32.5 percent, are poor, placing its poverty rate slightly above those of other rust belt cities such as Milwaukee and St. Louis, and slightly below troubled Detroit and Cleveland. Almost half, 42.9 percent, of its residents are African American.[11] Of DECA's approximately four hundred students, 84.6 percent are black; 74.5 percent are considered to be at the poverty level.

It's hard to know where to begin to describe the problems, given the interacting tangle of forces that trap so many children in their net, like the "throwaway kids," a term that DECA student Marquita[12] uses.

Orphaned Marquita's alcoholic grandmother rarely sent her to school, and when she did it was in dirty, worn clothes. It was only thanks to a caring principal that the child had any clothes at all. In the fifth grade, she spent many nights at a friend's house after Grandma shut her out of the house. Marquita would eventually live at Daybreak, a shelter for runaways, or for "throwaways," as she puts it.

Kaneesha was also a "throwaway." Kaneesha's mother had died when she was two, her father when she was four. The next seven years were spent with her dad's girlfriend, whom she called "Mom," until the latter decided she'd had enough of motherhood: the preteen would go into foster care. Next came a series of foster homes, which, says Kaneesha, would cause her to have "anger and depression."

Eighteen-year-old Daron's father "screamed and yelled and argued about everything," and the boy was always at odds with his abusive stepmother. Eventually his father threw him out of the house to fend for himself.

There are some who would say that Marquita, Kaneehsa, and Daron, born and raised at the low end of the socioeconomic scale, are fated for a lifetime of violence and poverty and of mind-numbing low-skilled jobs, if they are employed at all. But are they? The students at DECA, in our typical Midwestern city, with its typical inner city, are breaking the pattern and headed for success, in spite of their often dysfunctional upbringing. As Shawna, child of a crack addict, says, "This school, I think, has saved me. If I hadn't been here, with all that was going on in my life, I probably would have given up," thinking "maybe it's just not meant for girls like me to go to college."

How does DECA do it? Through a combination of what's been called "cuddles and challenges," nontraditional methods, and a culture that stresses cooperation among and between staff and students, even those as disadvantaged as Marquita, Kaneesha, Daron, and Shawna can realize their potential. What's more, as we'll see, there is much that other schools can emulate.

I was first introduced to the school when my husband Matt joined its board of trustees. Soon he was extolling its successes, especially with those students from disadvantaged backgrounds. The more I heard, the more I realized how important it was that their stories be told.

If it is possible to turn around the bleak picture of today's urban young people—and it is—this is a story well worth telling. And that's what *Breaking the Cycle* aims to do.

NOTES

1. Juan Williams, *Enough: The Phony Leaders, Dead End Movements, and Culture of Failure That Are Undermining Black America—And What We Can Do About It* (New York: Three Rivers Press, 2006), 73.

2. Abigail Thernstrom and Stephan Thernstrom, *No Excuses: Closing the Racial Gap in Learning* (New York: Simon & Schuster, 2003), 123.

3. Thernstrom and Thernstrom, *No Excuses*, 12.

4. Williams, *Enough*, 93.

5. Karl Weber, ed., Prologue, *Waiting for "Superman": How We Can Save America's Failing Public Schools* (New York: Public Affairs, 2010), 4.

6. William H. Cosby Jr. and Alvin F. Poussaint, *Come On, People* (Nashville: Thomas Nelson, 2007), 9.

7. Cosby and Poussaint, *Come On, People*, 109.

8. Thernstrom and Thernstrom, *No Excuses*, 56.

9. Cosby and Poussaint, *Come On, People*, 109.

10. Andrew Sum, Ishwar Khatiwada, Joseph McLaughlin, and Paulo Tobar, *The Educational Attainment of the Nation's Young Black Men and Their Recent Labor Market Experiences* (Boston: Center for Labor Market Studies, Northeastern University, 2007), 13.

11. Source: U.S. Census Bureau.

12. Some names and details have been changed to protect privacy.

Acknowledgments

My thanks first to DECA's students who felt it was important that they share what they have accomplished and who were eager to convince others that it is, indeed, possible to hurdle the barriers that poverty erects. Thanks, too, to the teachers, administrators, and all the DECA family, who never hesitated to take time from their busy days to tell me more about their remarkable school. I am also grateful to Terry Ryan of the Thomas B. Fordham Foundation for his help. Special appreciation is owed to Thomas Lasley II, DECA founder, supporter, and educator extraordinaire, who has taught me so much about what constitutes an effective school. May this book do justice to all those who share in this extraordinary story.

Introduction

As the woeful statistics reveal, growing up in the inner city sets up road-blocks to education that rarely exist in more affluent areas. Poor urban youth face myriad pitfalls that shape their future: drugs, violence, crime, fatherless homes, and, often, inadequate schools that fail to prepare them for life.

In this dark corner of our current reality, however, a few candles glow, and that is what *Breaking the Cycle* is all about. It highlights one of these candles, the Dayton Early College Academy, known as DECA. This school, in a quintessential Midwestern city, achieves remarkable success with children whom many would write off as doomed to failure: all its students are headed for college, where an astounding 84 percent will receive their degrees. And, notably, its efforts are largely replicable.

In the first section of the book, "Challenges," we examine the obstacles that urban students must face in their struggle to gain an education and access to a productive life. Through the eyes of the students themselves, we see the world in which they live, a world of which most middle-class Americans are largely unaware. DECA students graphically relate their own experiences with a world infected with drugs and violence.

We hear the stories of students like Shawna, who took responsibility for the children in the family while neglecting her own welfare, or Andre, the only one in his family not addicted to drugs, or LaShanda, traumatized by the violence in her home.

Although they credit their mothers for much they have accomplished, both girls and boys lament the absence of their fathers' love and protection. They often carry the burden of negative peer pressure, while they resent educational backgrounds that have left them far behind their suburban counterparts.

In the second part of the book, "Overcoming the Challenges," we look closely at the people, methods, and visions that have changed the course of the future for DECA students.

In a study of five of the world's best school systems, the Battelle Institute determined several factors that such schools had in common. Experiential and collaborative learning, mutual trust between students and teachers, high expectations, a focus on learning rather than accountability, attention to the whole individual, ongoing feedback, and ties to the community—these are the attributes of the world's best schools. Teachers also have a great deal of latitude in how they reach their goals.

As we'll see in this section, these qualities also shine through at DECA, where its unique "advisory" system creates a family, engendering trust, cooperation, and close parent–school relations.

Its rigorous academic program includes a series of "Gateways," with requirements that become progressively more demanding. In addition to classroom instruction, Gateways require completion of over one hundred hours of community service, two job internships, three job shadows, a twenty-page autobiography, three college courses, five in-depth research projects—complete with a PowerPoint presentation—twenty-one literary analysis papers, and a 95 percent attendance rate. Gateways are judged by an intimidating panel of teachers, parents, a board trustee, and, often, important visitors, to whose probing questions presenters must respond.

DECA students are not only prepared for higher education but are furnished with the "soft skills" of the professional world, those "cultural norms" required for successful careers. Students are also introduced to the college life that awaits them by taking college courses while still in high school.

Most importantly, much of what DECA does can be shared with the community. As Principal Dave Taylor says, "It's not about keeping secrets. It's really how do we improve our learning pursuits."

But establishing and operating a school like DECA has not always been smooth sailing. In chapter 10, "Bumps in the Road," we look at some of the problems encountered in its early days.

Nevertheless, the school has amassed an amazing record, bursting onto the educational scene with a rapid accumulation of awards. Based on a compilation of characteristics that top educators advise, a checklist of the qualities that DECA and other well-performing schools exhibit is included.

But there's more to the story. Not only do students progress in academics, but in character, as well, as they continue to give back to their communities.

Part I: Challenges

In this section we examine the obstacles that urban students must overcome in their struggle to gain an education that will lead to productive, fulfilling careers. As their personal stories breathe life into the cold statistics, we recognize that DECA students, too, are real people, not so different from those in more affluent areas, although they face challenges rarely encountered in the wealthier suburbs.

Chapter One

Drugs

In the poverty-stricken areas of America's cities, alcohol remains the substance most commonly abused. It was alcohol that led Tawana's father to steal the $500 she had saved for college. It was alcohol that led Marquita's grandmother to forget to send her to grade school—for 140 days out of the school year's 180—or to buy the growing girl new clothes, or even to wash the ones she had. And it was alcohol that led Ka'leigh's mother's boyfriend to practice his knife-throwing by aiming at Ka'leigh and her brother, missing them by inches as the terrified children stood against the wall. But it is drugs that seem to have eclipsed all other forms of substance abuse when it comes to destroying urban families.

There's no way to escape the drug culture if you grow up in the inner city. According to the sociologist Elijah Anderson, especially in what he calls the "hyperghetto," "everyone knows someone or knows about someone with a drug habit whose life has been impacted in some ways by drugs." [1]

Even if yours is one of the "decent families," as opposed to the "street families" that Anderson describes, you are bound to be affected. High school senior Andre describes how even the playgrounds in the park were taken over by addicts: "They were sleeping on the slides, so sometimes you couldn't even go slide, because some drug addict would be there, trying to get shelter."

The prevalence of drugs is more than an annoyance. Shootouts between rival drug gangs kill and injure many innocent victims every year. DECA student Taynor will never forget racing to the hospital with his wounded friend after an intergang dispute. Not long after that incident, ten-year-old Quayshon Hill was shot in the head in the parking lot of a restaurant when "bullets raked his mother's car" in a case of mistaken identity. [2] Even young children learn early on to be on the lookout for danger and steer clear.

It's worse when that culture enters the home itself, driving mothers to neglect and abandon their offspring. "In some of the most desperate situations," says Anderson, "the oldest children take over, procuring and preparing food and performing other household duties,"[3] as in Shawna's case.

Shawna is a beautiful girl who looks a little like a young Janet Jackson and who, like all teens, wants to look her fashionable best. Today she's wearing a purple shirt with a purple starburst over a blue, long-sleeved T-shirt, jeans, and boots, standard high school fashion. A little bit of lace peeks over the round neckline of her T-shirt, and she wears a silver necklace. She punctuates her thoughts with a soft nervous chuckle.

It's hard to believe that this lovely seventeen-year-old was once, as she writes, "a third-grade girl with flooding pants, shoes that were too small, hair that was beginning to fall out, and a dingy sweater," taunted by classmates for being dirty. She remembers winning the spelling bee competition and rushing home to show her mother her certificate when she ran into her on the street, walking from the corner where children were not welcome. Her mother, however, passed right by without seeing her, in a drug-induced trance and clutching a "hard white rock with a yellowish tint." Shawna tells more about her life:

SHAWNA'S STORY

My mother was twenty-seven when I was born. She had her first, my oldest brother, when she was twelve, and then two more after him, and then me, and then two more after me. She has been a drug addict, off and on, mostly on, and my father—I don't know who he is, he was just in town to have a good time, you know, partying. He never meant to get someone pregnant, so he doesn't know I'm here today!

My mother had me, I came into the world, and I did have crack in my system. My mother did use crack while she was pregnant with me. She kind of argued with the doctor. You know, of course, when a baby is filled with crack, you don't really want to give it to that parent, but somehow she ended up walking out with me, but they said I would cry a lot because I craved it, and so they would have to rock me.

Even now at times I think I never really grew out of it, because I still find myself, if I'm just sitting here, I will rock from time to time. I never knew where that came from, until my sister finally told me, "Well, when you were a baby, to get you to be quiet, we'd have to rock you, because, obviously, we couldn't give you a drug." So, that's it.

My mother was sent to prison when I was two. She went to Marysville, not for dealing, but using drugs and the things addicts do to get the drugs. So, she came home and then for five years she was clean and sober. I don't really remember her using drugs, because I was so young, because at age two you don't really know anything better.

My grandmother—actually she was my great-grandmother—took care of us while my mother was sent to prison when I was two. She was kind of like the rock of the family. When things went wrong, she was the one to make it right. And then, she passed away. I was eight when that happened, and that's when it collapsed—the stability, and everything I was used to: my mother being home when I got home, food in the refrigerator, lights and heat on, telephone on.

All of that just kind of collapsed then, and I found myself being confused by that, because I wasn't really used to those things. I was used to those five years when she was clean, and it took me a while to figure out that it was drugs that were the cause behind all of it.

Looking back on it, I was still clueless. I didn't know it was crack cocaine. I thought—I don't know what I really thought. I just knew she was never home. She would go sometimes six, seven days without coming home or calling. My oldest sister, Angie, who was sixteen at the time, took care of us then. When I was one or two years old and my mom was doing drugs, Angie was the one who potty-trained my brother and me.

My mother's mother, my grandmother, was on drugs, too. She actually used heroin and crack. And so I always wondered, "You saw what that did for her. Why did you do it?"

My great-grandmother was from Georgia, and she and her husband migrated to the North for better opportunities, but because of the cost of migrating the whole family, they decided to leave their children with a family member. Well, her daughter, who was my grandmother—she was raped and she got pregnant with my mother at twelve. So they sent my pregnant grandmother back up here to be with my great-grandmother, where she gave birth to my mom.

I think because it was a rape and she was so young, my grandmother really didn't want anything to do with my mother, so my great-grandmother took care of my mother, and then my mother got pregnant at twelve, not that she was raped. So when it came time for my older sister to become of age, I think my mother worried about her a lot, because it's kind of like it's a generational thing. Well, she got pregnant, but it was at sixteen, not twelve, not that there's much difference. She has two children now, and they're living at St. Vincent's homeless shelter.

I'm getting counseling. I worry a lot. Freshman, sophomore, and the beginning of junior year, I was an above average student. I've always had a percentage in the 90s, and it's never dropped from that. But my teachers knew I could perform so much better than that, but it's hard when you have a thousand things going on at home, so I was constantly worried. When I found out that my grandmother had died, which was like the very shaking of my foundation, they called me to the office, and we went home.

So now, every time I'm called to the office, I get scared, because I'm like, is there a police officer here to tell me that they found my mother dead somewhere? Is she in jail? Because when she goes six, seven days without even calling, you have no choice but to worry.

I allowed my mother to read my [school-required] autobiography. It was very much based on her. I don't feel like I bashed her in any way, like I didn't express any kind of hate, not that I don't feel . . . but I was truthful about a lot of things that she probably didn't know. She even approached me and said,

"Why didn't you tell me certain things?" And I said, "Mom, I did, but you were probably so high that you didn't understand." So she's not really happy with that bio . . .

I wrote that at one time I had been staying in a vacant house. That's one of the things she got very upset about. My mother was doing good at a point, but it seems that every time the Christmas season comes, it all falls apart. That's the season my grandmother died, two weeks before Christmas.

We were staying in a house, and then that season came, and she went crazy! She sold all of our things. My brother would have to cut holes in his box springs to hide his shoes, because he didn't want her to sell them. So it got really out of control. I think she has this mind-set that she can take money that she gets from the state and play with it or blow it, and she always has in the back of her mind that her children will help her. She always comes to us. It's almost as if we're her parents and she's our child.

She couldn't pay the rent, we had no lights in the house, there was no power, and if you do not have any lights or power, you are not allowed to stay in that house, especially if you have children. So they evicted us, and we had to go to St. Vincent's [homeless shelter]. But there were family altercations and a lot of family problems, so I couldn't be at St. Vincent's.

I had no other place to go, so I went back to that house. There was no furniture, there wasn't anything in there, and it was so cold and dark in there and everything. So by definition it is abandoned. Does she want me to change the word for it? I could say we weren't supposed to be in the house, but any other way, it was abandoned. We abandoned it to go to St. Vincent's homeless shelter because she decided she didn't want to pay the rent.

My family? I have three brothers and two sisters. My mom always made the statement that it was funny that her crack babies turned out to be better than the normal ones. My brother Joshua and I are the crack babies. Joshua's a year older than me. He never really got the chance to be the baby, because when he was like three months, she got pregnant with me.

We've always been very close. He's going to Sinclair Community College and working, and he's actually staying at Daybreak [the shelter for teens] right now, because my mother, once again, is evicted from her current house, but he's doing well, and I'm here, and I'm staying with my teacher, Mrs. A. And my oldest brother—he's thirtysomething, he's only had one job his whole life. He hasn't graduated from high school, and he stays where he can. He had that job for a year, and now he's just doing what he can to get by. He was at Sinclair, though, I will give him that.

My sister, she dropped out of high school—well, she just stopped going. There was never anyone there to tell her, "Get up and go to school." She got pregnant, and she's at the shelter right now.

My younger sister is also at the shelter with my older sister. I think my mom's just given up on being a parent. She doesn't want the responsibility. She's still on drugs. I think she's seeing that one by one we're all starting to go. First it was me, then Joshua, and then my sister. I don't think she has the desire to even be a parent anymore. Well, she's expressed that sometimes, which is a little hurtful to hear from your mom, but . . .

Melonie, too, has suffered from her drug-addicted mother's neglect. Once when she was ten, the girl and her little brothers had been left alone. It was not the first time, but this time when their mother didn't come back for days, the authorities entered the picture and the children were placed in foster care.

That wasn't the worst thing that had ever happened, however. That had been a few years before when Melonie was left at home with the new boyfriend while her mother went out for drugs. The man who had seemed so nice, who had helped her with her homework, and who had called her "a really good kid," dragged her into the bathroom and raped her. She was seven years old.

"When it was all over," she remembers, "all I could do was sit in my living room and wait until my mother got back. I sat in a curled-up ball in the corner, up against the wall. My knees to my face, not a single sound muttered, my heart slowly beating like I was dying. I just look in sorrow as if my soul had been ripped from my body."

Her mother had her daughter's assailant arrested, but he was found not guilty. Who would believe the young child of a drug-addicted mother?

* * *

Although drugs have been around for a long time and heroin is still a problem, it was crack that reached the epidemic stage in the 1980s. According to researchers Robert G. Carlson and Harvey A. Siegal, crack was known as early as 1976 in Dayton, but it became popular first on the East and West coasts, a popularity ironically increased by the attention given to actor Richard Pryor's free-basing accident in 1980.[4] Its use has given rise to a whole subculture with its own rules of business, job descriptions, and vocabulary.

Crack is a mixture of cocaine powder, enough water to moisten it, and baking soda. The mixture is heated until a ball forms, then cooled with ice water until it solidifies. Other substances may be added, such as yeast or 7-Up®, to expand it for more profit or to increase potency. Purity can range from 5 percent to 40 percent.

"Men who sell crack are called dopemen, boulder boys, servers or rock stars. Women who sell large amounts of crack are simply called dope women. In most cases, dealers tend to work in teams of two or three for mutual protection against rip-offs. Some dope men employ an armed doorman who has the job of verifying the sincerity of potential customers and weeding out suspected snitches."[5] Others in the business include "runners" who "rush" customers in exchange for crack, and owners of "smoke houses" or "geek houses," known as the "house man or lady, or simply as the house."[6]

Crack not only can cause mothers to forget their children and tear apart families. It can lead to hallucinations and paranoia, turn the body into a wizened shell, and make users "geeks" or "fiends." "It changes everything," says one addict. "It brings out the dog in a person. Makes you just don't give a damn. You'll stab your own brother or people in the back just to get another hit."[7] If you're smoking crack, "don't nobody care about their mamas. They just as soon kill their mama for crack."[8]

"Geeking" is what Carlson and Siegal define as "the myopic focus on self-gratification coupled with complete disregard for self and others."[9] Geeks will do anything to obtain more crack. It "involves a neglect of personal hygiene, a lack of self-respect, and a disregard for moral values and social norms," and it can lead to the most degrading sexual practices imaginable, all under the rubric of "personal favors."[10] It is not surprising that many crack users become AIDS victims.

For Andre, dealing drugs is the family business. The DECA senior, who has received a generous college scholarship, is the only one in the family who has never been addicted at one time or another. He's determined not to go down that path. He's proud that his family calls him "the One," after the leader in the *Matrix* film who was destined to save humanity.

ANDRE'S STORY

I come from a single-parent family. My father passed away when I was four years old. I have an older brother and a younger brother, and I have an older sister, also. My mom has three kids, my dad only had me and my sister, and my grandmother has six kids, so I have one auntie and four uncles.

All of my uncles right now are in jail. A lot of them have been in and out of jail for years, for drugs, theft, just a lot of unnecessary things that could have changed. Why did they do that? Most of them always tell me it's because they don't have a dad in their lives, that they always felt alone, but I didn't have a dad in my life and I'm doing well in my life, so that's not an excuse. It's up to you to make the choice, and they chose the wrong path.

I have a little cousin whose father isn't in his life at all, ever since he was born, so he looks up to me, and that's like my other little brother. My older brother has five kids. He's twenty-six.

All of my uncles have done drugs. My brother, he used to smoke weed, my mom used to smoke weed. My uncle actually went to jail for drug charges . . . My dad used to sell drugs before I was born. That's when he stopped selling them, when he had a child, because it was so dangerous.

I asked if it was hard for his family members to get a job after being incarcerated. What do ex-prisoners like them do after they get out? Do they go back to selling drugs?[11]

My uncles do, but my dad had a heart problem, so physically he wasn't able to work anyway, and that's why he sold drugs, to provide for his family and everything like that. He was caught with sixteen grams of cocaine in the car, but because he had a good lawyer, he only got a year and a half. My uncles who are going to jail, it's hard for them to get jobs, and I've noticed myself, watching them try to get jobs. One of my uncles tried to get a job at McDonald's, but he couldn't work there because he had a felony.

Selling drugs can be a felony, but it depends on the amount that you actually get caught with. My uncle had a murder charge, because he was driving under the influence and crashed into a car and killed an eight-year-old boy when he crashed into the car, so he was charged with that.

For my uncles, even when they get back out of jail, they have friends who sell the drugs who join up, and it's not hard to get drugs in the community. I mean, it's processed everywhere. My uncles know how to make drugs in their own kitchen, making cocaine into crack.

Although Andre says his uncles started dealing drugs "just to provide," they soon became addicted to their product, which led one of his uncles to steal his elderly mother's medications. "My grandma has a lot of things wrong with her, and she takes a lot of pills. My uncle stole her Vicodin and sold them. But my uncles have stolen in general. One of my uncles stole the first game system I had when I was little, because he wanted to feed his addiction. Another one stole his child's piggybank to buy drugs also."

According to Bryson, another student, "a lot of younger kids are selling drugs because it's the cool, popular thing to do." But sometimes, he adds, it becomes an economic necessity. "Most of us here are poor, so we have to help provide for the family, so a lot of students use that as an outlet to provide for families."

As civil rights attorney Michelle Alexander says, "Suburban white youth may deal drugs to their friends and acquaintances as a form of recreation and extra cash, but for ghetto youth, drugs sales . . . are often a means of survival, a means of helping to feed and clothe themselves and their families."[12] Elijah Anderson agrees that families sometimes have to rely on the money from drugs: "It becomes even more difficult to separate the drug culture from the experience of poverty."[13]

Today it is prescription drugs that have become the major problem, says Dr. Robert G. Carlson of Wright State University's Center for Interventions, Treatment and Addictions Research (CITAR). Again, sometimes it's a question of economics. "It's not unknown," he says, "for elderly people in particular to purchase medications legitimately for health problems, or antidepressants or benzodiazepines: Ativan, Xanax, and so forth. And then they can sell those and make a significant profit. And for elderly people on fixed incomes that can be a significant operation."

He adds that

now, with cell phone technology, people sell drugs over the phone. Someone will get a bunch of drugs and say, "Hey, I've got ten Percodans for so much money. Who wants them?" And somebody else will say, "I need Oxycontin. Where can I get it?"

> With pain pills, people don't understand what they're getting into. College kids go out to a bar and they know if they take a Vicodin, they won't have to buy as much beer, because a few beers will increase the effects of the Vicodin tablet that the person took. [Oxycontin] leads to dependence very quickly. And the expense of purchasing Oxycontin can become overwhelming.

And so addicts have turned to heroin, which is cheaper, "because the feeling will be very similar to Oxycontin." Of course this drug dependence leads to stealing and other criminal means to maintain the habit.

Nor do users understand the dangers. In our local county alone, in 2010 there were 130 deaths from accidental overdoses, and there were similar numbers in the two preceding years. [14] The problem is no longer restricted to the inner city but is one that "has grown rapidly, especially in rural regions." [15] Today drug overdoses are the leading cause of accidental death throughout the country, exceeding traffic fatalities. [16]

Just as Shawna and her brother were born addicted to crack, more and more babies are entering the world craving Oxycontin or other medications. "As prescription drug abuse ravages communities across the country," according to the *New York Times*, "doctors are confronting an emerging challenge: newborns dependent on painkillers."

Babies like three-day-old Matthew, who are born addicted, "may cry excessively and have stiff limbs, tremors, diarrhea and other problems that make their first days of life excruciating. Many have to stay in the hospital for weeks while they are weaned off the drugs, taxing neonatal units and driving the cost of their medical care into the tens of thousands of dollars." Little is known yet about the long-term effects on their development. [17]

A new drug on the scene is so-called bath salts, a hallucinogen responsible for several deaths locally in recent months. Dayton's Miami Valley Hospital has seen an average of one case a day during the same period from this over-the-counter substance, available at head shops and gas stations.

* * *

Why do people turn to drugs in the first place? For Tonya, baby Matthew's mother, "it was a lot easier to get through life and have energy" while she worked the overnight shift at an industrial bakery an hour from her home. [18] For many, says Carlson, it is because they have no hope for the future. They look to drugs to relieve the despair of poverty. Teens might bend to peer pressure—it's the "cool" thing to do. Some, like Andre's uncles, blame the lack of a father figure, the right kind of role model.

Harlem educator Geoffrey Canada explains how drug dealing became so attractive for the younger generation. It was in the mid-1970s, he says, that young people, usually male, began to enter the drug trade. He blames the unintended consequences of the so-called Rockefeller drug laws, enacted under the New York governor of that name, for this "new employment market."

Older dealers knew that under the new, harsher laws they might be faced with severe punishment, even lifetime imprisonment. With the juveniles, however, judges were much more lenient. And so drug dealers came up with an answer that "was as simple as it was evil. They began to use children."[19]

It would prove irresistible to those young people "whose lives [were] haunted by tattered clothes, empty refrigerators, broken dreams, nerves of steel, and toughened hearts." What is more, neighborhood drug dealers often provide the only role models for boys, who "associate the power and wealth of the drug dealer with making it as a man."[20]

Now the children would have vast amounts of money at their disposal. Too young to invest in cars, homes, or businesses as older dealers would, however, they bought "designer clothes, expensive sneakers, and gold jewelry," which, of course, they would have to protect. And so handguns, once relatively rare, now became a common possession among young people. All of which would lead to more violence in an already violent environment.[21]

NOTES

1. Elijah Anderson, *Code of the Street: Decency, Violence, and the Moral Life of the Inner City* (New York: Norton, 1999), 28.

2. *Dayton Daily News*, "Suspects Sought in Shooting of 2 Children," April 16, 2011.

3. Anderson, *Code of the Street*, 28.

4. Robert G. Carlson and Harvey A. Siegal, "The Crack Life: An Ethnographic Overview of Crack Use and Sexual Behavior among African-Americans in a Midwest Metropolitan City," *Journal of Psychoactive Drugs* 23, no. 1 (January–March 1991): 12.

5. Carlson and Siegal, "The Crack Life," 12.

6. Carlson and Siegal, "The Crack Life," 13.

7. Carlson and Siegal, "The Crack Life," 15.

8. Carlson and Siegal, "The Crack Life," 16.

9. Carlson and Siegal, "The Crack Life," 15.

10. Carlson and Siegal, "The Crack Life," 16.

11. For an exposition of how the War on Drugs and the criminal justice system actually exacerbate drug problems and poverty, see Michelle Alexander, *The New Jim Crow: Mass Incarceration in the Age of Colorblindness* (New York: The New Press, 2010).

12. Alexander, *The New Jim Crow*, 209.

13. Anderson, *Code of the Street*, 29.

14. Ben Sutherly, "Local Accidental Drug Overdose Deaths Twice as Much as Similar Ohio Counties," *Dayton Daily News*, January 27, 2011.

15. Sutherly, "Local Accidental Drug Overdose Deaths."

16. *Los Angeles Times*, "Drug Deaths Now Outnumber Traffic Fatalities in U.S., Data Show," September 17, 2011, www.articles.latimes/com/2011/sep/17/local/la-me-drugs-epidemic-20110918.

17. Abby Goodnough and Katie Zezima, "Newly Born, and Withdrawing from Painkillers," *New York Times*, April 10, 2011.

18. Goodnough and Zezima, "Newly Born."

19. Geoffrey Canada, *Fist, Stick, Knife, Gun: A Personal Story of Violence* (Boston: Beacon Press, 1995; rev. ed. 2010), 78.

20. Canada, *Fist, Stick, Knife, Gun*, 78.

21. Canada, *Fist, Stick, Knife, Gun*, 81.

Chapter Two

Violence

Ten-year-old Quayshon Hill was not the only child endangered in shootings in the spring of 2011. Within less than a week of when shots were fired at the Hill family's car, there was what police considered a related shooting, possibly in retaliation for the earlier incident. This time it was a six-month-old baby who narrowly escaped death. While the baby slept in a bedroom with her mother, a barrage of gunshots blasted the house where she lived. Her grandmother, in the living room, was struck in the leg. [1]

And in our local paper, another violent incident so common as to seem almost routine: three teenagers, including a fifteen-year-old girl, were arrested for the murder of a young man for his bicycle. Willie B. Tottie III was shot and killed as he rode home from a friend's house.

According to the National Center for Post-Traumatic Stress Disorder, "Over one-third of girls and boys across the country ages 10 to 16 years are victims of direct violence," and "even more children have faced indirect community assault. That is, they have seen violence or they know a victim of community violence. Over three-quarters of children in a high-violence urban area reported coming into contact with community violence."

The risks increase when children live in poor, inner-city areas, are non-white, are in a gang, use alcohol or drugs, or experience domestic violence. [2] In a study of 246 inner-city youths in Detroit, 44 percent reported that they could obtain a gun within a day, 41 percent had seen someone shot or knifed, and 22 percent had seen someone killed. [3] In another study, "only 12% of inner-city adolescents indicated that they had not been exposed to violence," the remaining 88 percent being more subject to depression, suicidal behavior, and posttraumatic stress disorder. [4]

What is now termed "posttraumatic stress disorder," or PTSD, following exposure to violence was first clinically described after World War I, when

13

symptoms like "persistent and frightening recollections, flashbacks, and constant anxiety" indicated what was then called "shell shock syndrome."

Veterans of all wars apparently have suffered from such reactions, but not long ago it was thought that, because of their immaturity, children would soon recover from such events. Not so, say Angelo Giardino and his fellow medical researchers, who have found that chronic PTSD can even lead to changes in "brain microarchitecture."[5]

Giardino, clinical associate professor in the Pediatrics Department of Baylor College of Medicine, and his coauthors discuss the emotional and physical effects of violent experiences on children: "Although some children may be genetically resistant to PTSD, "nearly all children who witness a parental homicide, approximately 90% of sexually abused children, 77% of children exposed to a school shooting, and 35% of urban youth exposed to community violence go on to develop PTSD."[6] Along with sleep problems, hypervigilance, and emotional numbing, traumatic experiences can lead, especially in males, to "conduct disorder, antisocial behavior, and/or criminal behavior following significant violent trauma,"[7] ironically repeating the cycle.[8]

In a National Institutes of Health (NIH)-supported study under the direction of Dr. J. Douglas Bremner, he and his Yale colleagues conclude that "childhood abuse and other extreme stressors can have lasting effects on brain areas involved in memory and emotion. The hippocampus is a brain area in learning and memory that is particularly sensitive to stress."[9] Thus they claim that education itself may be affected:

> The effects of childhood memory and the brain also have important implications for public health policy. This is especially pertinent for inner-city children who often witness violent crimes in their neighborhoods and families, in addition to trauma, such as childhood abuse. If abused children have damage to brain areas involved in learning and memory, this may put them at a serious disadvantage that programs such as Head Start will not be able to overcome. Consistent with this, traumatized Beirut adolescents with PTSD had deficits in academic achievement, compared to non-traumatized adolescents and traumatized adolescents without PTSD.[10]

Such effects on the brain can directly influence school performance, says Paul Tough, author of *How Children Succeed*: "Children who grow up in stressful environments generally find it harder to concentrate, harder to sit still, harder to rebound from disappointments and harder to follow directions."[11]

Andrew Williams, who heads Retrak, an organization working with street boys in Uganda, agrees that trauma can affect the brain and its functions: "Trauma . . . has been shown to restrict functioning in the thinking and problem solving part of the brain that controls emotional response," he says.

"Challenging behaviour by children who have experienced trauma may have psychological roots we need to be aware of."[12]

John A. Rich, a physician with a master's degree in public health, sees similarities between those who suffer from a violent environment and those with posttraumatic stress syndrome from the battlefield, the same hypervigilence, the same jumpiness.[13] And a virtual battlefield it is. "Up to 45% of people who have had a penetrating injury—a gunshot or stab wound—will have another similar injury within five years," and 20 percent will be dead.[14]

The death rate for young black men aged fifteen to thirty-four is nineteen times higher than that for white men of the same age. As one teenager says, "You step on someone's foot or look at somebody the wrong way—if he doesn't like your attitude, he might pull out a gun and kill you."[15] How stressful it must be to follow the street code, as rigid as any samurai's *bushido* creed. Rich repeats what he has learned from a seventeen-year-old gang member named Jimmy:

- If you want to avoid being a sucker, you have to have a rep.
- If you want to have a rep, you have to earn it.
- You earn a rep by putting in work.
- In Jimmy's world, work means doing violence.
- Having a rep, even if you got it by violence, makes you known.
- You could get a rep for doing good, but people might still come after you for disrespecting them in the past. Therefore, violence is more effective.[16]

In other words, gaining respect is "a form of self-defense."[17]

Rich has joined with others to meet victims of violence where they are perhaps most accepting of change—at the hospital where they are treated for injuries. He has been instrumental in founding and maintaining support groups for such victims in several large cities.

It's no wonder that Martha Brzozowski, DECA's onsite mental health therapist, worries about her charges. "When I worked in residential, where kids lived there, at least I knew they'd be taken care of," she says. "Some of these kids, though, I worry when they go home. It's just amazing the things they have to go through. An example, a kid might get held up at gunpoint over the weekend, or someone knows somebody who got shot. It's not uncommon. Or they get in a fight with their mom, so now they're living with an aunt. Or they don't have to a place to go, so I'll try to get them in touch with Daybreak, the shelter for teens. They just have so many things that they're dealing with."

DECA students are well aware of the dangers of their community, and some claim to have been very fortunate to have avoided the ever-present violence, much of which has been gang involved. According to the *Dayton Daily News*, in spite of a law-enforcement campaign that has sharply reduced street crime, some seventy-seven gangs with 948 known members continue to be a threat in the city. [18]

Damarion admits he has friends who are gang members, but he has managed "not to get wrapped up in the hype of being in a gang . . . I just decided I didn't want to maybe lose my life over a color or a sign." Those who live life on the streets, he says, and "do what they're doing now," will eventually get themselves killed or end up in jail. In the meantime, he knows that in his neighborhood, "violence goes on. I'm not fearful," he claims, "but at the same time I keep an aware mind that even though I'm walking in my neighborhood, something can still happen to me, so I just try to be cautious and make sure I watch my back."

For Andre, gangs and their violence have not been a problem, thanks to his older brother's "rep." Although he sees gang members "a lot," they don't bother him, he says, "because my brother was in gangs, and a lot of people know him, so no one really tries to mess with me because they know the way he is."

Daron has also benefited from being in the shadow of his older brother. "I've had a lot of contact with gangs," he says.

> I'm really happy about one thing that has proven to be effective. My brother went to [a school with a work-study program], where there are a lot of gangs. They get along for the most part at school, at the job site, but there are lots of gangs at that school.
>
> Now my brother is not affiliated with a gang, however, he's the kind of person that can talk to everybody, so he can create the community, bring the community together. From the little I know, it has a very, very, very, very good triple effect, because when I walk through neighborhoods, 99.9 percent of the time, they say—because my brother and I look alike—"Are you Tyrone's brother?" "Yes, I'm Tyrone's brother." "Hey!"
>
> It's more a friendship, more like a good communication. It's not like, "Yeah, we're going to jump you." It's more like, "Oh, where are you headed to? You want us to walk with you?" kind of thing. It has created a kind of protective shield when I go to certain neighborhoods.

I asked cheerful Jewanna if she worried about members of her large family becoming involved with gangs. She replied: "This is how we all stay out of it. My mom isn't a people person. If you met her, she would talk to you, but wherever we live, we stay to ourselves. We don't know our neighbors. My mom doesn't want to get to know anyone. We're always at home. We never go anywhere. I'm seventeen, and I've never been anywhere."

Jewanna is "amazing," I was told by other students, for she is always smiling, in spite of poverty even more severe than that most of the students experience. "I get by on my personality," she says. For this friendly senior, who is definitely the "people person" her mother isn't, the isolation must be especially hard. (Jewanna is a big girl with a heart to match her size. When a scheduling conflict prevented her from joining a school outing to the King's Island amusement park, she gave the money she had saved up for the trip to someone who hadn't been able to afford it.)

"In my community, my neighborhood," says her classmate Jolena, "there are a lot of things that go on. Kids do get shot up." Girls are aware that they are not immune from the dangers, and they often learn to protect themselves. She adds:

> I have seen gangs and groups of people doing violent things. I experienced one of them doing that to a student here. I was at the bus stop. A group of DECA kids were at the bus stop one day, and a gang of boys decided just to pick on one person, and they started hitting him. Most of the people were scared and they were like backing away, just standing there, but I chose to jump in and help. I'm an amateur boxer, so those things are not like a big deal to me . . .
>
> I don't think it is fair that one person should just be bullied by some— especially if he didn't do things. They don't know him, and they were just trying to find some way to stir up some trouble, so that's what they did. Other people started to help after I jumped in, and then they just ran off. There were no adults around to help whatsoever . . .
>
> Eventually they started to have police officers stay at the bus stop to make sure that nothing would happen to anyone.

Among the "hidden rules" for surviving in poverty, no matter what your color might be, Ruby K. Payne, an expert on the culture of poverty, cites knowing "how to fight and defend [oneself] physically."[19] Martha Brzozowski, DECA's mental-health therapist, believes that it is important to know about conflict management, but she recognizes that the students may indeed have to stick up for themselves in some situations.

She says, "I try to teach the kids that that same skill set that you can use, say on the street or in your neighborhood, is not going to work in all settings. When you go to work and you go to college, that set of skills is not going to work for you, so I try to teach them, 'I'm not taking that away from you. Don't try to say that that's not what you need, but you need to learn something else for different places.'"

For Jolena and her fellow students, their school is a safe haven from the violence, unlike the public school that Dannisha's cousin attends, where he was able to bring a gun in with him, in spite of security guards and a metal detector.

Although young women are at risk, it is young black males who suffer most from the violent environment. Imagine the stress of always having to "watch your back," and, as the sociologist Elijah Anderson says, "be on one's guard constantly."[20] Young men know that "violence can come at any time, and many persons feel great need to be ready to defend themselves."[21]

Shawna worries about her younger brother, who she fears "is on that trail. It saddens me," she says, "but he has this need to be violent for some reason, and I wish he could be put into football, or maybe boxing, even, to perhaps channel that violence."

DECA students share their insights on why young black men, especially, are at risk of falling into the temptations of gang membership and its violent culture.

Bryson agrees that those in trouble need better role models. "All they see," he says, "is these people selling drugs or doing bad things." Alonzo, a DECA graduate now a full-scholarship student at a prestigious school, says "it hurts" when he sees the kinds of lives some of his former neighborhood friends are living. They "know that there is something missing and they're longing for something, but they find it in all the wrong places, such as drugs, sex . . . I think they're trying to find some kind of acceptance."

"Gangs are a major problem in my environment," says LaTonya:

> It's shameful because you are living a negative life mainly because you want that attention and you're looking for it in the wrong place. You just want that structure and that foundation, which is not wrong. It's not wrong to want that foundation and that family life . . . A lot of the time gang members have that mentality that "this is always going to be my family," so when you get in your forties and fifties, what are you going to do? Will you still be doing the same thing? I have an uncle—he still has that gang mentality, so even if you leave the gang, there's still some way to have that mentality, I guess.

According to James D. Rowell, in an article in *Police: The Law Enforcement Magazine*, "Gangs grow because the gang provides kids with basic human needs. These include the need for security, love, friendship, acceptance, food, shelter, discipline, belonging, status, respect, identification, power and money."[22] Gang leaders "prey upon the need of young people to belong and to be recognized," PBS television's Tony Brown agrees.[23]

Young black males historically suffer from a sense of powerlessness.[24] Add to this the "deep-seated rage" about inequitable poverty cited by Cornel West, the black activist and Princeton professor, and it's no wonder that a nihilistic environment exists among poor black Americans.[25]

Nor do inner-city residents trust those who are supposed to protect them. In general, says Elijah Anderson, "there is a profound lack of faith" in the judicial system—and in others who would champion one's personal security.

> The police, for instance, are most often viewed as representing the dominant white society and as not caring to protect inner-city residents. When called, they may not respond, which is one reason many residents feel they must be prepared to take extraordinary measures to defend themselves and their loved ones against those who are inclined to aggression. Lack of police accountability has in fact been incorporated into the local status system: the person who is

believed capable of "taking care of himself" is accorded a certain deference and regard.[26]

He found that in the Philadelphia neighborhood in which he conducted research, the police would often witness drug dealing, yet "seem indifferent to the dealing or they sometimes abuse the very residents they are supposed to protect."[27] It's almost a given that racial profiling exists: a common "offense," inner-city residents say, is for "DWB": "driving while black."

The O. J. Simpson murder trial highlighted how many African Americans feel about law enforcement in the United States. It was not until the famous football star was acquitted of murdering his wife that whites got "a clear look at the depth of black alienation from the criminal justice system."[28] One DECA board member, who was serving on another board of trustees at the time, remembers how the members were evenly split by race. The whites were incredulous; the blacks, jubilant. Perhaps too many of the latter had once found themselves unjustly accused.

* * *

Many blame the violence among black males on the lack of good role models, as DECA students do. When boys grow up in fatherless homes, they may look for father figures who are close at hand: the drug dealers, gang leaders, and other criminals. The kinds of men who once provided stability for the neighborhood are no longer around. The civil rights era opened up new opportunities for black community leaders, allowing them to leave the segregated areas in which they were once obliged to live.

Others fault the influence of television on growing minds. According to the Kids' Health Organization, "The average American child will witness 200,000 violent acts on television by age 18. Kids may become desensitized to violence and more aggressive. TV violence sometimes begs for imitation because violence is often promoted as a fun and effective way to get what you want."[29]

American children watch a lot of television, which also means less time for studies, as well as constant exposure to desensitizing displays of violence. African American children watch even more than their white contemporaries do, according to Abigail Thernstrom and Harvard's Stephan Thernstrom: "Nearly half of African-American fourth-graders spend *five hours* or more staring at a TV screen on a typical school day"; less than one-fifth of the white children devoted that much time to television viewing.[30]

It is also "startling and dismaying," they say, "to discover that close to half of all black eighth-graders watch television for what must be more than a third of their waking hours on school days." Even in high school, when academic demands are greater and many hold part-time jobs, "nearly one-third of all African-American students were still watching television for five hours or more."[31]

It's a situation that Bill Cosby and Alvin F. Poussaint also decry. "Here is something we all know: there is too much violence on TV—even on cartoons. Child-care professionals believe that kids who are exposed to a lot of violent media are more likely to use violence. The older they get, the more they see, the more violent they get."[32]

Indeed, researchers have found a significant correlation between those who watched a great deal of television violence as children and those who showed aggression as adults. In a longitudinal University of Michigan study, "Men who were high TV-violence viewers in childhood were convicted of crimes at over three times the rate of other men."[33] Others blame the media, too, for promoting a materialistic culture in which the latest fashion is worth stealing, maybe killing for.

Some look to history for explanations. The sociologist Thomas Sowell in his book *Black Rednecks and White Liberals* claims that violent behavior of Southern black men was at least in part due to their imitating the behavior patterns of white Southerners who came from the turbulent culture of pre-eighteenth-century Ulster, the borderlands between England and Scotland, and the Scottish highlands.

"More is involved here than a mere parallel between blacks and Southern whites," Sowell asserts. "What is involved is a common subculture that goes back for centuries, which has encompassed everything from ways of talking to attitudes toward education, violence, and sex."[34] He adds that "centuries before 'black pride' became a fashionable phrase, there was cracker pride—and it was very much the same kind of pride," a "touchiness about anything that might be even remotely construed as a personal slight, much less an insult, combined with a willingness to erupt into violence over it."[35]

Although Thomas Sowell traces the roots of black violence back to seventeenth-century America and before, fellow conservative John McWhorter traces many of the problems of inner-city communities to the late 1960s. Antiestablishment attitudes of the hippy generation joined with generous welfare programs instituted in those liberal times would lead to "a permanent transformation of the group mind-set of the black community."[36] He explains that "a new culture emerged of white-hot, unfocused animus against mainstream culture."[37] Now one could survive without working, and "blacks who rejected mainstream norms were accepted as normal rather than 'characters' or 'layabouts.'"

One way to create "a violent underclass culture of lax parenting, casual violence, and widespread substance abuse," he maintains, is "to institute a program that leaves thousands of mothers with no reason to work and a father with no reason to take responsibility for their offspring."[38]

Drugs had been on the scene for a long time during the period he's concerned with. That's a given. But why, he asks, was it only after the 1960s that people were so open to using them?[39] He argues that *"poor blacks have indeed been waylaid by a culture of poverty."*[40]

For this self-destructive behavior, fueled by black insecurity, McWhorter coins the term "therapeutic alienation," which he defines as "alienation unconnected to, or vastly disproportionate to, real-life stimulus, but maintained because it reinforces one's sense of psychological legitimacy, via defining oneself against an oppressor characterized as eternally depraved."[41]

It's the kind of alienation that has led to the "sociopathic" and misogynistic music of such rappers as Ice Cube, Li'l Kim, Tupac Shakur, and 50 Cent, who sang that if a woman sticks around, she must understand that he is into "havin' sex—I ain't into makin' love."[42]

Bill Cosby blasts the media that only present women as sexual objects, the music videos being the worst. Women are commonly referred to as "hos and bitches." A CD by Young Gotti is "an evil trifecta—sex, drugs, and violence—all on one action-packed CD."[43]

Male loyalty is to the peer group, not to the mother of his child, says Elijah Anderson, and "the more the young man seems to exploit the young woman, the higher is his regard within the peer group."[44] Bakari Kitwana notes that when Tupac Shakur allowed his friends to gang rape his date and defended them, he was showing loyalty to his friends, not to the female victim. "This type of in-group male loyalty has emerged as a cornerstone in young black male culture," he says.[45]

According to Anderson, "The lore of the streets says there is a contest going on between the boy and the girl even before they meet. To the young man the woman becomes, in the most profound sense, a sexual object. Her body and mind are the object of a sexual game, to be won for his personal aggrandizement. Status goes to the winner, and sex is prized as a testament not of love but of control over another human being."[46]

Many of the men in a study conducted by William Oliver, assistant professor of criminal justice at Indiana University, as well as a board member of the Institute on Domestic Violence in the African American Community, "associated manhood with dominance of one's woman and children."[47]

In the face of such male attitudes, African Americans are affected by a disproportionate number of violent incidents between partners, according to Minnesota's Institute on Domestic Violence in the African American Community: "In 2005 African Americans accounted for almost 1/3 of the intimate partner homicides in this country"; "Black women comprise 8% of the U.S. population but in 2005 accounted for 22% of the intimate partner homicide victims and 29% of all female victims of intimate partner homicide." And rates of teen dating violence were almost twice as high among black youths

as among white teens (almost 14 percent versus 7 percent of those sur-
veyed).[48]

"As with other abusive men," the institute says, "African American men
who batter are higher in jealousy and the need for power and control in the
relationship."[49] Economic factors are also to blame. A seventeenth-century
adage says that when poverty comes in the door, love goes out the window;
poverty greatly increases the rate of violence in the home, as does the use of
alcohol.

It is a sad fact of life that many poor black men, frustrated and impotent in
their poverty, have "directed most of the anger, rage and despair toward
fellow black citizens, especially toward black women, who are the most
vulnerable in our society and in black communities."[50]

Domestic violence is particularly pernicious for children, affecting them
in the very place where they should feel safe. DECA student Monica remembers what her mother's boyfriend was like, as she wrote for a school assignment:

MONICA'S STORY

*I was eight when my mom moved out. She had been living in a trailer park for
about a year when Wendell decided to hit her. Punch, hit, kick, and push. One
time I stayed the night at her trailer, and he went ballistic.*

*I was outside, playing in the dirt and trash-infested black top when I heard
her voice: "Monica! Come inside right now, it's getting dark." . . . Wendell
and my mother were in the living room arguing. Wendell started throwing
things, hitting walls, and slamming the aluminum door. His eyes were blood-
shot from all of the alcohol and smoke that had soaked into his body. He smelt
of old beer and looked as if he had just gotten beaten up, including his sweaty,
clinched face and wadded fists.*

*It scared me, but I just stayed back in the bedroom alone, with the door
shut. Even after the abuse, my mom still chose to be with him over me and my
father. At that moment I lost all compassion and love for her. I never felt the
same about her after that; I hated the very thought of her.*

Monica's experience was bad, but her classmate LaShanda's was worse,
as she described in a writing assignment for school:

LASHANDA'S STORY

*When I was ten, everything began to take a turn for the worse. I saw my
parents constantly fighting or arguing about something. It really bothered me
because I would wonder what was going to happen to my family.*

One night I heard a loud slam of the door. The loud slamming of the door came from my dad in the middle of the night. When he came in, I heard him yelling loudly at my mother.

CRASH. "You've been messing around again, huh?" He said. "I'm always out working all these late hours and I got to come home and hear you've been messing with this other dude!"

"No, Dillon, I haven't!" she yelled repeatedly, muffling between strikes from my dad.

"DAD stop!" I yell. "She's been here the whole time."

"Go to your room, LaShanda."

"No, Dad, STOP!" From the struggle of the words he was trying to get out, I noticed he sounded like he'd been drinking.

"Where's the TV, Shauntel, did you sell that too?"

Screaming: "Dad, the TV's in the room. Please STOP. You're hurting her!"

Immediately I saw his fist slam into her face, blow after blow after blow. Although I wanted to cry, I was frozen in fear to see my mom being beaten. I couldn't do anything to help her. I was so frozen in fear that every step I took forward, I cried. After he hit her numerous times, he picked her up off the couch, and a big gasp of air left my mother's body.

"Dillon, stop please!"

My dad slammed her up against the corner of the wall. Again he slams her, but this time through a window.

CRASH! All the glass shattering into a million pieces, but he didn't care about what he was doing. It was like watching a horrific car accident and all the car's windows disappearing all at once because of the impact.

After slamming her through a window you'd think that he was done, but he wasn't. He threw her out the door.

"Get out!"

Severely traumatized by the blood splattered up against the walls and on the floors, I watched him pick up a sheet and begin to wipe up the blood off the walls and floor, two feet from me. A couple of minutes later I heard police sirens getting louder and louder. I prayed that nothing would happen to me or my parents, but it did.

I look out the window as my dad is being taken away in the back of a police cruiser. Dad? I thought as I watched my mother slowly walk up the driveway after the police drive off.

I tried to help but she wouldn't take it. She headed to the couch in the living room, blood stained and all. "Go back to bed."

The pattern of violence might be carried down through the generations. As DECA grad Vanetta observes:

If you have a destructive home life, or you have someone who is verbally abusive or physically abusive and you don't have those resources to get help, or to even have the resources to speak about it, it ultimately can lead you down a self-destructive path. And I always say, "hurting people hurt people," and that's a cycle, as well. If I'm hurting, I'm more likely to hurt others. You see it a lot of times when you look at the statistics for domestic violence, in that normally they grew up in a domestic violent home themselves or some sort of abuse.

Jolena believes that "crimes are committed, violent crimes" for the same reason that young women have babies at a young age. "I think that the majority of that stems from lack of love, lack of attention. I think that starts in your home."

Was it a coincidence that the sixteen-year-old charged with Willie B. Tottie's murder over his bicycle was found by the police nine years before alone with his two-year-old sister in an apartment with no food, clothing, or furniture?

NOTES

1. *Dayton Daily News*, "Retaliation Shootings Put Children in Danger," April 19, 2011.

2. U.S. Department of Veterans Affairs, "Effects of Community Violence on Children and Teens," National Center for PTSD, www.ptsd.va.gov/public/pages/effects-community-violence-children.asp.

3. H. Schubiner, R. Scott, and A. Tzelepis, "Exposure to Violence among Inner-city Youth," *Journal of Adolescent Health* 14, no. 3 (1992): 214–19, www.ncbi.nlm.nih/gov/pubmed/8323933.

4. Ideation, Depression, and PTSD Symptomatology," *Journal of Abnormal Child Psychology*, 27, no. 3 (1999): 203. James J. Mazza and William M. Reynolds, Exposure to Violence in Young Inner-city Adolescents: Relationships with Suicidal Ideation, Depression, and PTSD Symptomatology," *Journal of Abnormal Child Psychology* 27, no. 3, 1999.

5. Angelo P. Giardino, Tol Blakeley Harris, and Eileen E. Giardino, "Child Abuse and Neglect, Posttraumatic Stress Disorder," July 28, 2009, www.emedicine.medscape.com/article/9160007-overview.

6. Giardino, Harris, and Giardino, "Child Abuse and Neglect," 3.

7. Giardino, Harris, and Giardino, "Child Abuse and Neglect," 2.

8. Giardino, Harris, and Giardino, "Child Abuse and Neglect," 2.

9. J. Douglas Bremner, "The Lasting Effects of Psychological Trauma on Memory and the Hippocampus," www.lawandpsychiatry.com/html/hippocampus.htm.

10. Bremner, "The Lasting Effects of Psychological Trauma on Memory and the Hippocampus," 5.

11. Quoted in Annie Murphy Paul, "School of Hard Knocks," review of *How Children Succeed*, by Paul Tough, in *New York Times*, August 23, 2012.

12. Andrew Williams, *Working with Street Children* (Lyme Regis, UK: Russell House Publishing, Ltd., 2011), 49–50.

13. John A. Rich, *Wrong Place, Wrong Time* (Baltimore: Johns Hopkins University Press, 2009), 95.

14. Rich, *Wrong Place, Wrong Time*, xi.

15. Jonathan Kozol, *Amazing Grace: The Lives of Children and the Conscience of a Nation* (New York: HarperPerennial, 1995), 47.

16. Rich, *Wrong Place, Wrong Time*, 57.

17. Rich, *Wrong Place, Wrong Time*, 65.

18. Steve Bennish, Kelli Wynn, and Doug Page, "One Local Gang Maintains Power, Influence in City," *Dayton Daily News*, March 10, 2012.

19. Ruby K. Payne, *A Framework for Understanding Poverty*, 4th rev. ed. (Highlands, TX: Aha! Process, Inc., 2005), 38.

20. Elijah Anderson, *Code of the Street: Decency, Violence, and the Moral Life of the Inner City* (New York: Norton, 1999), 37.

21. Anderson, *Code of the Street*, 42.

22. James D. Rowell, "Kids' Needs and the Attention of Gangs," *Police Magazine*, June 1, 2000.

23. Tony Brown, *Black Lies, White Lies* (New York: Morrow, 1995), 14.

24. Edward T. Hall, *Beyond Culture* (New York: Anchor, 1989), 5.

25. Cornel West, *Race Matters* (Boston: Beacon Press, 1993), 5.

26. Anderson, *Code of the Street*, 34.

27. Anderson, *Code of the Street*, 30.

28. David K. Shipler, *A Country of Strangers: Blacks and Whites in America* (New York: Knopf, 1997), 375.

29. "How TV Affects Your Child," KidsHealth, www.kidshealth.org/parent/positive/family/tv_affects_child.html.

30. Abigail Thernstrom and Stephan Thernstrom, *No Excuses: Closing the Racial Gap in Learning* (New York: Simon & Schuster, 2003), 142.

31. Thernstrom and Thernstrom, *No Excuses*, 142–43.

32. William H. Cosby Jr. and Alvin F. Poussaint, *Come On, People* (Nashville: Thomas Nelson, 2007), 139.

33. L. Rowell Huesmann, Jessica Moise-Titus, Cheryl-Lynn Podolski, and Leonard D. Eron, "Longitudinal Relations between Children's Exposure to TV Violence and Their Aggressive and Violent Behavior in Young Adulthood: 1977–1992," *Development Psychology* 39, no. 2 (2003): 201–21, 210.

34. Thomas Sowell, *Black Rednecks and White Liberals* (New York: Encounter Books, 2005), 1.

35. Sowell, *Black Rednecks and White Liberals*, 7.

36. John McWhorter, *Winning the Race* (New York: Gotham Books, 2005), 63.

37. McWhorter, *Winning the Race*, 63.

38. McWhorter, *Winning the Race*, 69.

39. McWhorter, *Winning the Race*, 108.

40. McWhorter, *Winning the Race*, 112.

41. McWhorter, *Winning the Race*, 6.

42. McWhorter, *Winning the Race*, 340.

43. Cosby and Poussaint, *Come On, People*, 49.

44. Anderson, *Code of the Street*, 154.

45. Bakari Kitwana, *The Hip-Hop Generation: Young Blacks and the Crisis in African-American Culture* (New York: Basic Books, 2002), 101.

46. Anderson, *Code of the Street*, 154.

47. William Oliver, *The Violent Social World of Black Men* (New York: Jossey-Bass/Wiley, 2001), 83.

48. Institute on Domestic Violence in the African American Community, www. Dvinstitute.org.

49. Institute on Domestic Violence in the African American Community.

50. West, *Race Matters*, 18.

Chapter Three

Single Mothers

Over 70 percent of black babies are now born to single mothers. [1] We may wonder why this figure is so high when there are so many advantages to two-parent families, not the least of which is financial: in 2002, "single-parent families were roughly five times more likely to be poor than two-parent families." [2] In our local five-county metropolitan area, 40 percent of single mothers are living in poverty. [3]

The case for not marrying has many arguments. To begin with, for many black women, good husband material is hard to find. Although some men might want to "make babies" to assert their skewed idea of manhood, those same men apparently are less willing to make a full and lasting commitment to the mothers of those children.

Kitwana blames the hip-hop culture for the "throwaway mentality" that so many black men exhibit toward women. "Central to our identity," says this African American scholar, "is a severe sense of alienation between the sexes." [4] Why should a woman marry a man who thinks, like "Lee," a black male of the inner city, that "man is dominant"? He describes male attitudes in the ghetto: "Man rules. The man should be the one able to make his say-so and it be that. Give no say-so to a woman. Put no value on how she feels about any situation or anything." [5]

Chances of a happy marriage seem remote when for many men the object of a relationship is just "to hit and run while maintaining personal freedom and independence from conjugal ties," as the sociologist Elijah Anderson maintains. Out for "instant gratification, some boys want babies to demonstrate their ability to control a girl's mind and body." [6]

And so, according to Bill Cosby, "some black women simply don't want to marry the father of their children because these men appear to have little else to offer beyond the sperm. Many of these men are unemployed and unemployable."[7] Or in jail. Jacqueline Jones concluded in her research that "poor black communities had a uniquely high sex-ratio imbalance, reflecting the relatively large numbers of young black men either incarcerated or killed by violent means."[8] Prison culture only intensifies the rift between the sexes.[9]

Having a baby is not always a conscious decision. In the culture of poverty, in which one lives for the moment, seldom does the young woman (or man) consider the consequences[10] or think it's possible to make choices that could change the way things are in the here and now. "An underlying cause of pregnancy," says Anderson, "is a lack of a sense of future."[11]

Middle-class teens have the same raging hormones, but most of them "take a stronger interest in their future and know what a pregnancy can do to derail it. In contrast, many inner-city adolescents see no future that can be derailed—no hope for a tomorrow much different from today—hence they see little to lose by having a child out of wedlock."[12]

Andrea Parrot confirmed this in a study conducted by Cornell University: "Too many teenage girls see themselves as having nothing to strive for—they can't see graduating from high school because they have few role models to follow, their teachers give them little encouragement about their abilities, their families are chaotic and their friends are on drugs. Parenting looks like the best thing going, many girls think, because babies provide an immediate source of unconditional love."[13] Very young people know little about birth control, anyway.[14]

Many of the poor put a lot of faith in fate,[15] and religion may even play a part, for, as Anderson says, "One reason [for teen pregnancies] may be the strong fundamentalist religious orientation of many poor blacks, which emphasizes the role of fate in life."[16]

DECA graduate and college senior Jewel thinks that "you just get caught up in the moment. That's really it. Everybody always has that mentality, 'It won't happen to me,' and when it does, it's kind of a shock. You thought you could beat the system [and not get pregnant]. You know, it's kind of like playing Russian roulette. But they don't really see it that way."

According to her friend and fellow DECA grad Vanetta, unplanned pregnancies are due to "looking for love in all the wrong places." When you grow up in poverty, she says, "you have a lot of holes and gaps, and sometimes you use different substances or different patterns, even though they're destructive, to medicate, whether it be sex, whether it be alcohol or drugs."

"That peer pressure, that's the biggest thing," Bryson says. "I think it goes back to sex is the cool thing out there these days. If you're not doing it, you're not in the in crowd."

Girls may want to have a baby in order to hang on to its father. "Becoming pregnant can become an important part of the competition for the attentions or even delayed affection of a young man," which, says Anderson, is "a profound, if socially shortsighted, way of making claims on him."[17] It's a situation with which DECA senior LaTonya, who mentors younger girls, is familiar:

> I have many friends who unfortunately have become pregnant. I want to say, based on what I have seen and the connections I have made to young girls who have been pregnant, basically one of the main aspects is that they are ignorant. Because a lot of times they have the mentality, "OK, if I give this man or this boy what he wants, then he'll give me the attention that I need."
>
> A lot of the time they're not thinking about the consequences, because the consequences of them giving their attention and giving their body to a man in return for his attention is bearing a child that neither you nor the other person wants.
>
> It's very difficult because these young mothers who are so ignorant, basically, are having these children when they're children, and they don't know the ropes, so how can you show your child that? So a lot of the time you're just going with a mother who is basically just going with the flow because she doesn't know what to do. They're so young. How can you raise a child when you're struggling to take care of yourself?
>
> I can give an example. There was this girl recently who I was mentoring. She's fifteen, and she wants to have a baby with this guy, because she wants him to be with her, and so basically she didn't take the necessary precautions to stop that. She did the opposite in order for her *to* get pregnant, but instead she didn't, so she lied about it, so that he can still some way be with her, because she's telling him that she's pregnant, but she's not.
>
> And he's like, well, "I'm about to have a child." No, you're not about to have a child. She's not freaking out. She's basically going with the flow. She's happy because he's around, but he's freaking out because he's so young, he doesn't know what to do.
>
> He's nineteen now, just turned nineteen, and she's fifteen. At first he didn't know she was fifteen. He thought she was eighteen, but she lied about her age. So when it all came out that she wasn't pregnant, they created that distance, because that's not the situation you need to be in. A fifteen-year-old young lady does not need to be focusing on having a child. You're still a baby! You don't need a baby.

Having a baby is not altogether a negative thing. For most women, young or old, babies are adorable. We want to hold them, cuddle them, feel their warm bodies close to ours. The maternal instinct is a powerful force. For men, too, "the human instinct to create new life, to nurture and love and be loved, cannot be overcome except by formidable hopelessness."[18]

The generous welfare policies of the 1960s and 1970s made having a child more affordable; the period of more liberal sexual mores led to the end—or at least a diminishing—of the stigma of unwed motherhood.

For many young women, "motherhood . . . becomes a rite of passage to adulthood."[19] Having a baby can prove one's worth, Anderson says, since a large part of the mother's identity is provided by the baby. He sees it as a question of pride: Since babies are extensions of their moms and "reflect directly on her," members of the "baby club" compete as to which baby is the cutest and best dressed, often buying expensive clothes for their offspring. "'Looking good' negates the generalized notion that a teenage mom has messed up her life, and amid this deprivation nothing is more important than to show others you are doing all right."[20]

According to Anderson, "becoming a mother can be a strong play for authority, maturity, and respect," even though it limits a young woman's choices.[21] "Typically," he continues, "a young girl with a limited outlook and sense of options for the future is easily enlisted for [the mothering] role. In conditions of persistent poverty, she may look forward to the rewarding roles of mother and, by extension, of grandmother."[22]

The strong single mother is an important factor in the community—and at DECA. Says Judy Hennessey, superintendent, "The strength of these women to hold their families together, to work multiple backbreaking jobs, to find a way to pay for the bare necessities and still come to our parent meetings, and still be on their kids—it's amazing to me. . . . I look at some of these women, and I can't help but be inspired by them, even though they had babies that they couldn't afford, and they allowed men to be in their lives who weren't helping them, but there is this resilience and strength that you just can't help but admire."

Many students are grateful to their mothers for much that they have accomplished. Alonzo, a DECA grad and now a junior at a prestigious college, credits his mother with his accomplishments. "Strong and tough," she had a vision for him:

> She was a strong individual who raised me the way I was supposed to be raised. My dad was a drug dealer and he wasn't really around. It was just me, and my mom and my sister. I knew everybody [in the gangs], but at the same time I was able to stay true to what I believe in, and not conform to my environment. I think my mom did a great job when she raised me. She not only told me not to do [something], but she would explain why you shouldn't do it and how it would affect you.
>
> I think if parents today would tell the kids why, it would be an instrumental part in them actually changing, 'cause if somebody told me I couldn't do it, and gave me no explanation behind it, it would probably make me want to do it even more, but my mom—and I thank her for it every day—she explained, "You shouldn't do this, because this will happen and this will lead to that, and those are the consequences behind it."
>
> So when I heard the consequences, I was like, "No, I'm not going to do that,"—like when people ask me to drink, smoke, I say, "No, I'm not going to do that. My mom raised me . . ." I actually say, "I'm crazy enough to believe my mom."

LaTonya, who plans to be an attorney, describes her mother as "truly phenomenal":

> My father has been incarcerated for sixteen of the eighteen years of my life, and because my mother had her first child at sixteen, she was unable to obtain her high school diploma. However, she does have a trade degree. She has her state-tested nursing certificate. She went to Sinclair Community College and finished there. She does in-home health care . . .
>
> I have a big family. I have six sisters and four brothers. My mother, she only has four children. However, my father, he has the large number of children, but my mom took on that motherly role to all of my siblings, because we were all close in age and she wanted my sisters and brothers and me to have that close relationship. So many times my sisters and brothers would come to stay with me if they had problems with *their* home life, with their mother. I have a big connection with my brothers and sisters because of my mother.

Alonzo describes his family: six sisters and one brother. "My brother's adopted, as well as in my mother's home we take in foster children. We have one that's staying with us a while. In my home I live with just my mom. My mom and dad are separated. My sister is in college right now. My other sister, she's grown. She's working. She has a child. It's basically me, my mom, and my little brother, but the house is always full. My niece is always there. My mom is like the glue that holds the family together."

The tradition of the strong black woman can be traced back through centuries of history. Patrick Moynihan blamed oppression and slavery for what he called the "pathology" of poor black families in the 1965 "Moynihan Report," which angered civil rights leaders.[23] "It was by destroying the Negro family under slavery that white America broke the will of the Negro people," Moynihan claimed, leading to the cycle of poverty and family instability that still exists today.[24] Under slavery, fathers could be separated from their families, leaving the women in charge.

Even deeper roots of black women's strength, however, can be found in certain areas of West Africa, where, according to the historian Betty M. Kuyk, "women and men are of equal worth."[25] In the Bight of Biafra region, from which many American slaves came, "inheritance. . . was matrilineal." Because of this, [the clan's] princesses were important and held a political voice." Kuyk also describes a female in an early slave community in South Carolina who was very powerful, "functioning as the head of her people" and controlling "workers, drivers, and white overseer alike."[26]

In the times of slavery and sharecropping, white men did not consider black women to be as much of a threat as black men, says Elijah Anderson, and so women "were then allowed to develop into strong, independent, willful, wise, and omniscient matriarchs who were not afraid to compete with men when necessary."[27]

Inner-city African American women possess a special spiritual strength, too. As Jonathan Kozol wrote about one urban area of New York: "It is true that there are many little miracles and thousands of heroic people in Mott Haven, and not all of them are children who like Edgar Allan Poe or adults who write poetry. Many are simply strong, resilient mothers and grandmothers, some of them devout black women, in whom Cornel West has rightly said one often finds a spiritual strength unknown to most other Americans."[28] God gives them strength, says Anderson.[29]

Alonzo is also grateful to his mother for the religious faith that sustains him; he remains "spiritually grounded" as he faces the challenges of college. Like many inner-city women, she is a devout Christian. "Going to church, shirt and tie, all of that, he says, laughing, "that was from my mom!"

Among the poor, "the mother is always at the center of the family," says poverty specialist Ruby K. Payne, but it is the grandmother who is traditionally the backbone. Samovar and colleagues note that in its African-based respect for the elderly the black culture differs from that of mainstream America, for "the role of grandmother is one of the most central roles in the African-American family."[30]

According to history professor and award-winning author Jacqueline Jones, "The West African tradition of respect for one's elders found new meaning among African Americans. For most women, old age brought increasing influence within the slave community."[31] Anderson agrees that the grandmother is "an extremely important source of support for the black family, the anchor holding in place the family and indeed the whole kinship structure."[32]

Today, although she may be quite young—typically in her mid-thirties or early forties—"she is once again being called upon to assume her traditional role," as "with the loss of well-paying manufacturing jobs and the introduction of drugs (particularly crack) and the violent drug culture into the ghetto . . . the heroic grandmother comes to the aid of the family, taking responsibility for children abandoned by their own parents, asserting her still considerable moral authority for the good of the family, and often rearing the children under conditions of great hardship."

She, too, gains strength from God, especially if she is called upon to raise her grandchildren. "God is love, wisdom, eternal life. Taking care of your grandchildren is all part of this. . . . You may not be able to save your daughter, but you can save your grandchildren," says Anderson,[33] but he fears that as time goes on, there will be fewer to take their place.[34]

It was Granny who taught her "many life lessons," Kristol says.

> The biggest lesson my Granny taught me was my love for God. She has an overwhelming love and commitment to God. My mom was never really a strong believer in God, but my Granny, on the other hand, tried to instill those

values into my sister and me. She wanted us to get an understanding of God so well that we spent the night over at her house every weekend so that we could go to church on Sunday. She even bought us church clothes so that when we did go to church, we would look the part.

Going to my Granny's house was a vacation away from all the violence of [my bad neighborhood]. My Granny had an actual house with a yard. I had never lived in a house before. My Granny lived in a neighborhood which was a very different atmosphere from where I lived with my mom. We had the opportunities to go fishing with my Grandpa, fly kites, make snow men and all types of things that kids could do that lived in houses. We even helped her plant flowers and wash the car. Most people take these things for granted, but my sister and I saw it as a privilege. . . .

It also felt good to have two parents. I had a grandmother and grandfather that were married. They were the only married people I knew. They had a stable, committed relationship that was not always portrayed to me in real life, but only on television.

Other students also tell of the special closeness to their grandmothers. Damarion is a future medical student who, with his sister, was raised by their widowed grandmother, as was Karmon until her mother married Karmon's stepfather, and as was Daron for most of his life.

Daron says it was his grandmother who always told him after his mother died that "it's OK to show your emotions. And as I watched my grandmother, I learned that there were certain things that she did not like, that there were some things that she had to do that she did not want to do. However, she did them anyway, which is what I do. There are things that I don't want to do, but I do them anyway . . . I stayed with her a great portion of my life and I consider her the foundation of my character and my personality."

Ka'leigh's grandmother, she writes, "taught me my ABCs. She was my best friend. During our many times hanging out together we would have tea parties almost every day. . . . I loved my grandmother, and I think she took special care of me because she had always wanted a daughter. . . . Though I only have this handful of memories of her, she was still very influential and unforgettable."

The loss of a beloved grandparent can be devastating, as in Shawna's case, when she lost "the rock of the family," or when Karmon lost "the only person who made life worth living, success worth achieving, love worth loving."

David K. Shipler, journalist, Princeton professor, and prize-winning author, remarks that when the father is absent, a "realignment of family ties" takes place for many: "The extended universe of 'significant others' that includes grandmothers, grandfathers, aunts, uncles, siblings, and the web of caring that frequently—though not always—replaces the bonds of fatherhood. As grave as it is, the decline of the traditional two-parent household does not in every case mean the decline of nurturing love."[35]

Even with strong mothers and loving extended family, however, the absent father is missed. In addition to the financial problems that statistics show are suffered by households headed by single women, according to Brown University's James T. Patterson, children growing up in such households have more difficulties in school and more emotional problems than do their contemporaries from two-parent homes.[36]

Abigail and Stephan Thernstrom agree. They claim that "growing up in a single-parent, female-headed family 'is almost always associated with lower educational attainment and more behavioral and psychological problems.'"[37]

As Patterson reports, "Children growing up in impoverished single-parent families were far more likely than those in two-parent families to exhibit high dropout rates, low scores on educational achievement tests, high rates of teen pregnancy, significant problems with personal health and emotional development, high rates of criminal activity, and idleness and unemployment in early adulthood,"[38] or, put another way, "A two-parent home is less likely to be poor, and the children it produces are much less likely to end up in prison."[39]

Girls, as well as boys, need a father. As Anderson says, single mothers' daughters are especially vulnerable. He explains how it is in the ghetto, even for families that are trying to be "decent," because "in domestic situations where there is only one adult—say a woman with two or three teenage daughters—the dwelling may be viewed . . . as an unprotected nest." He adds that "in such a setting a man—the figure the boys are prepared to respect—is not there to keep them in line. Girls in this vulnerable situation may become pregnant earlier than those living in homes more closely resembling nuclear families," especially if the mother is away working long hours, leaving them without supervision.[40]

The statistics bear this out. According to one study, "Girls whose fathers left either before they were born or up to age 5 were seven to eight times more at risk of becoming pregnant as an adolescent than girls living with their fathers. A father's departure between ages 6 to 13 suggested a two to three times greater risk of becoming pregnant."[41]

The DECA students agree that without a father in the home girls are more likely to become pregnant. As Alonzo says, for things to change, "I know the household definitely has to get stronger, because I know that that happens in a lot of instances when the father isn't around, and I notice that the young ladies, it seems like when the father isn't around, they don't have the standard of what a male should be, so they accept anything that comes in, and if anything that comes in isn't a good male, that's all they know."

Alonzo's reaction to his cousin's pregnancy proves how important a father is thought to be, for Alonzo is shocked at the news. His middle-class, scholarship-college-student cousin does indeed have a good father. "It's funny," he says. "I never understood how you could be raised in a household when you have both parents, and especially when you have a father like my uncle is, and then you go and have a baby by who she had a baby by. I don't know how to fix the issue."

What is more, a girl needs a father for emotional reasons. Vanetta's father, who "wasn't around in the beginning," is one of the few who have actually managed to turn his life around. "My dad, when he was younger, was an alcoholic and a drug addict," she says, "and then he cleaned his life up and now he's actually an evangelist. He's very open about his past and how all those things made him learn. I'm so blessed to be able to have a relationship with my father, because when he wasn't there, I suffered a lot from low self-esteem, from just looking for love in the wrong places. . . . My dad—it means a lot to me to have my father admire me."

In an open letter to her father that Natasha wrote as a school assignment, she says:

> *Dear Father,*
>
> *I hated you at one point in my life. I hated you for not being the father I wanted you to be. I hated you for not being the father that I wanted to save me from this cold world. I hated you for starting a new family and leaving my sister and me out of your new family portrait. . . . I hated you for giving up on our lives to pursue your own.*
>
> *I just wanted your attention. I thought some attention from you would help you realize me. I was truly mistaken. I should have known you were never going to change. I remember when I used to stare out the window in the back bedroom of our townhouse. As the different cars would go by, I used to wish that one of those cars would be yours. I used to imagine that you were coming to surprise us. You just could not stop thinking about us and came because you had to pick up your girls! Just coming to get us simply because you missed us. For as long as I stared into the street and the oncoming cars, your car never showed up. . . .*
>
> *There were so many times when you cancelled on us. You were either too busy, work or something came up, and you couldn't make it, or you just simply didn't show up. Go figure, right? I used to be so upset that I would cry. I cried because of the disappointment. . . .*
>
> *This last summer, when I moved into your house, made this letter easier to write. Coming to live with you wasn't my first choice. It was more likely my last pick. My options were slim to start with. I really didn't want Mom to move out of town, but she needed to get away and start over. . . .*
>
> *So Mom came up with the proposal that I live with Grandma, who didn't have room for me, or with you. I didn't want to live with you because I knew I wasn't going to fit in, I wasn't going to fit into your household. Living in your house, those weren't the best conditions, but they weren't the worst. But then having to leave because of your house being constructed without any room for me was a turning point.*
>
> *Finally you could realize the father that I've witnessed for the last 18 years. Finally you realized how much it affected me, and how I communicate. Finally you apologized, and that's all I ever wanted.*

Sincerely,
Your Daughter

The year that Karmon was in the eighth grade was an especially hard time for her. That was the year her grandfather died, and the year after she was supposed to meet her father "for the very first time.'" Here, as she writes it, is:

KARMON'S STORY

I had heard his voice over the phone, read his handwriting from the letters he had occasionally sent, and had even known the type of cologne he wore that he sprayed on a bear he sent me. But I had never seen the man who had given life to me. Maybe he did not believe I was his child. Apparently my mother's confident and truthful testimony wasn't reassuring enough for him, so he took a paternity test. Obviously statistics didn't mean much to him either because 99.98 percent didn't make him be a father to me either.

The most painful story that my mother has told me about my father, more painful than the broken promises and denial of our natural bonding, was the first time he saw me. My mother and I were at a bus stop in Dallas, Texas, in the rain and he offered us a ride. I was three months old. Therefore, I figured meeting him in St. Louis would be the beginning of a fresh start. A chance for him to make it right. A chance for me to hear his side of the story; not to imply that my mother was lying, but for me to analyze what was running through his head after the announcement of my birth and I became a fully living human.

Needless to say, St. Louis wouldn't be my opportunity to receive those answers either. To add guilt to disappointment, my mother missed out spending quality, valuable time with her father in his last year on earth because she took me to the place my father had proposed to meet. I have never forgiven myself. . . .

All those years, no matter what he did or did not do, regardless of the many nights I cried to my mom from his broken promises, I wanted my father. I wanted to be Daddy's little girl. I wanted to cry to him when I was hurting and know that he would be there to make it better. I wanted to go to him when my mom wouldn't let me have my way and know that he would overturn her decision, and she wouldn't complain, because I was my Daddy's child. I wanted him to be there on my first date. I wanted him to cuss out my boyfriend the first time he hurt me. I wanted him to be there. I wanted my Daddy. . . .

I remember when I found out about my dad. Bobby Jackson, who I thought was my father, was not. I had never seen my biological father or met him. Bobby, the man I thought was my father, was never there for me . . . he never had time for me.

[My father] never knew where I lived, never came to my house, never saw me play basketball, and I love basketball. There was a time when I wanted to see my dad, there was a time when I didn't care if I saw him or not, and then there are times like this when I want to just be with him like a father and

daughter are supposed to do. I just want to spend days or weeks at my father's house, by my choice and not by force.

It's like I wanted to establish a relationship with my father, but I'm already a teenager and if we don't have a relationship now then I feel it's too late. I'm about to be a young adult soon. He missed out on all the things he should have been there for, like my first time riding a bike and things like that. . . .

I do want to start over so that I will be able to have a father figure in my life. I have men in my life but no one that takes full responsibility for me. Every once in a while somebody comes along and wants to act like my father, when truthfully they only want to be my father for the day or week, but there's nobody who has been there for me for a long period of time.

It would be nice for someone to help me with basketball or drop me off at practice, just to take me to a local park and play with me . . . I just want to have somebody just as interested in basketball as I am and support me . . . but really just to have a person who really cares for me and loves me. I just want him to fully support me in everything. I don't want him to force me to change, but accept me for me.

Truthfully I don't know what I want. It's like if I meet him, what will he be like? Will he be mean or really nice? Will we have an automatic connection or will it be awkward? What I am really afraid of is I am going to get close to him but then somehow he starts to distance himself from me. I'm scared that I will get attached and then I will lose him. The reason why is because I have been hurt many times before by people who come into my life and somehow disappear.

As Karmon hesitates over meeting her father, afraid that he, too, will disappoint her, she decides that she has nothing to lose, since "I'm at one of the lowest points in my life right now, and the only way to go is up from here. This may be a start to my happiness. I didn't know, but if I don't try I will never know."

So finally I met him. Today was a normal day, nothing new or extraordinary. I went to school and basketball practice. By 7:00 p.m. it was dark outside and I was lying in my bed when someone unexpectedly knocked at the door. . . . Surprisingly it was for me, but it was an unfamiliar face that I did not recognize.

He was slightly taller than me: about 5'9" or 5'10." He was cleanly shaven. He gave the appearance that he had just shaved before he came over. He was freshly dressed with a nice leather coat and when he spoke, he had a smooth, deep voice. He was a handsome man, a man you would be proud to claim.

My mom told me some minor details about my own dad. I did not have a large knowledge of him. He was very quiet and soft-spoken when he was younger. He was a good kid, but hung out with the wrong crowd. He never fully used his potential. He was a bright young man but was never challenged to excel and use his mind entirely. . . . His face was serious but somewhat nice.

He had a young face; he didn't look very old. He had warm and welcoming eyes. They were the color of hazel nut, a perfect brown. . . .

I tried to match his physical features with my own. He was pigeon-toed and walked as I did. We had very similar traits. We looked very similar and his mannerisms modeled some of my own. He had a strong, muscular body like he cared enough about his health to go to the gym and actually act on his nutritional goals.

And so Karmon discovered a new family and a father who, unlike Bobby Jackson, actually cheered her on at basketball games.

Many other days continued like this: fun, wonderful and surreal. I never thought someone you just met could make you feel more loved than family members that you have known all of your life. Someone who makes you feel welcome and important. Someone who walks into your life, not even fully sure that you are his child but makes you feel as if he birthed you himself, like you came from him. These are the things my dad did for me; all these things, and I have barely known him.

I just can't even really explain what the two years with my dad were like. He is now incarcerated for drug-related issues. He has been in jail for about a year now. If he could be at my graduation party, he would be so proud of me. He wouldn't be able to do anything but smile.

Boys, especially, need their dads, someone to tell them what to do[42]—or, "kick their butts," as some DECA young men put it. Even the best-adjusted young men resent the absence of their fathers.

Marcus, now a student at an Ivy League college, seldom sees his father. In the five weeks that he was in Dayton for summer break, he saw him once. He used to be angry that his father was never there, but now he is motivated to be a better father when he has a child. And although Marcus does see his father, he's not sure where he lives—"somewhere in Huber Heights, I don't know."

When he was growing up, his dad "was never really around," says Alonzo, a DECA grad now in college.

Because I have the same name as my dad, and I always felt that I would take pride in being the second, for the longest time I would hold grudges about why he wasn't around in my life. I know when I was younger, getting good grades, playing sports, I thought that would get him to come around, but it didn't. For a long time I just held a grudge against him, but then I came to DECA . . . and I was able to fill that void and it was easier for me to let go of that grudge and just love him and understand him.

There wasn't anything I could do. I did my best, and so now it's funny, like I can talk to him. I feel just fine. I don't hold anything against him . . . Sometime I'll just talk to my dad. I can just have a conversation now. No anger, no anything toward him. Nothing but love. I think a part of growing is you have to learn to get over the things that sometimes you don't want to, because it doesn't do anything, except just hold you back at the end of the day. Me holding a grudge against him is not going to help me in any way, it's not helping him. It's just lost energy, and at this point in my life I don't need any loss, I need all gain, positive energy.

Love there may be from female family members, but still, according to Dannisha, a boy needs a father:

What you think about when you see a gang on the outside looking in, you see violence, you see a group of misfits causing a bunch of mayhem and chaos in the neighborhood, but . . . how many young men do you know who live in an urban environment and have a mother *and* a father at home? And, more importantly, the father. Who else can define a man than a man, so if the father is absent, then who do they look to show them, "You are a man."

And while everybody says that a woman can raise a son, I wouldn't disagree. I think that women do a wonderful job of raising their children on their own, but let's just be honest here. There are some things that a woman just cannot do, and one of them is be a man, and so I think that gangs present that family, that bond between men that you can only find either between a son and a father or between a son and someone that they consider a father.

So it is that boys turn to "father figures" like gang leaders, or, as Shipler says, "oddly—the parole officer sometimes becomes uncle, older brother, pastor, teacher, coach."[43]

Even if black men avoid their children for fear that they would be bad role models, Bill Cosby pleads, "Claim your children," because "if you do not come to claim your children, you have stolen their hope. You have stolen any kind of feeling that they are worth something. They will have no sense of the past, little pride, and even less faith in the future. They will see fathers at the mall or on TV and they will wonder how stupid or ugly they must be to have driven their fathers away."[44]

NOTES

1. William H. Cosby Jr. and Alvin F. Poussaint, *Come On, People* (Nashville: Thomas Nelson, 2007), 14.

2. James T. Patterson, *Freedom Is Not Enough: The Moynihan Report and America's Struggle over Black Family Life from LBJ to Obama* (New York: Basic Books, 2010), 192.

3. Cornelius Frolik, "Jobless Rate for Single Moms at 25-Year High," *Dayton Daily News*, November 12, 2011.

4. Bakari Kitwana, *The Hip-Hop Generation: Young Blacks and the Crisis in African-American Culture* (New York: Basic Books, 2002), 6.

5. William Oliver, *The Violent Social World of Black Men* (New York: Wiley/Jossey-Bass, 2001), 69.

6. Elijah Anderson, *Code of the Street: Decency, Violence, and the Moral Life of the Inner City* (New York: Norton, 1999), 147.

7. Cosby and Poussaint, *Come On, People*, 14.

8. Jacqueline Jones, *Labor of Love, Labor of Sorrow: Black Women, Work, and the Family, from Slavery to the Present*, rev. ed. (New York: Basic Books, 2010), 289.

9. Kitwana, *The Hip-Hop Generation*, 83.

10. Ruby K. Payne, *A Framework for Understanding Poverty*, 4th rev. ed. (Highlands, TX: AHA! Process, Inc., 2005), 53.

11. Anderson, *Code of the Street*, 319.

12. Anderson, *Code of the Street*, 149.

13. Cornell Science News, qouted in Susan L. Lang, "Most teens get pregnant on purpose because other life goals seem out of reach, says Cornell researcher," June 4, 1997.

14. Anderson, *Code of the Street*, 177.

15. Payne, *A Framework for Understanding Poverty*, 52.

16. Anderson, *Code of the Street*, 147.

17. Anderson, *Code of the Street*, 156.

18. David K. Shipler, *A Country of Strangers: Blacks and Whites in America* (New York: Knopf, 1997), 561.

19. Anderson, *Code of the Street*, 147.

20. Anderson, *Code of the Street*, 165.

21. Anderson, *Code of the Street*, 148.

22. Anderson, *Code of the Street*, 210.

23. Paul Tough, *Whatever It Takes: Geoffrey Canada's Quest to Change Harlem and America* (Boston: MarinerBooks/Houghton Mifflin Harcourt, 2008), 27.

24. Quoted in Patterson, *Freedom Is Not Enough*, 48.

25. Betty Kuyk, *African Voices in the African American Heritage* (Bloomington: Indiana University Press, 2003), 53.

26. Kuyk, *African Voices in the African American Heritage*, 31.

27. Anderson, *Code of the Street*, 207–8.

28. Jonathan Kozol, *Amazing Grace: The Lives of Children and the Conscience of a Nation* (New York: HarperCollins, 1995), 160.

29. Anderson, *Code of the Street*, 218.

30. Larry A. Samovar, Richard E. Porter, and Edwin R. McDaniel, *Communication between Cultures*, 7th ed. (Belmont, CA: Thomson/Wadsworth, 2010), 73.

31. Jones, *Labor of Love, Labor of Sorrow*, 14.

32. Anderson, *Code of the Street*, 206.

33. Anderson, *Code of the Street*, 218.

34. Anderson, *Code of the Street*, 236.

35. Shipler, *A Country of Strangers*, 332.

36. Patterson, *Freedom Is Not Enough*, 180.

37. Abigail Thernstrom and Stephan Thernstrom, *No Excuses: Closing the Racial Gap* (New York: Simon & Schuster, 2003), 132.

38. Patterson, *Freedom Is Not Enough*, 193.

39. Cosby and Poussaint, *Come On, People*, 242.

40. Anderson, *Code of the Street*, 161–62.

41. Colin Allen, "Absentee Fathers and Teen Pregnancy," *Psychology Today*, May 1, 2003.

42. Allen, "Absentee Fathers and Teen Pregnancy," 174.

43. Shipler, *A Country of Strangers*, 352.

44. Cosby and Poussaint, *Come On, People*, 27.

Chapter Four

"Acting White"

Why do DECA students achieve at school when so many others don't? The college-bound students claim they're not super smart. They just work hard, and they're determined. But there must be something special about them when they can endure the peer pressure they get *not* to succeed. It's not unusual for LaTonya to get singled out in her neighborhood for comments like, "Why do you think you're so good?" she says.

A lot of times I've been called white, because I was able to compose sentences. I get that because, living in the society that I live in, especially being in an African American environment, there are low expectations placed upon me. And so breaking that and saying that I am more than the expectations it's like, "Oh, she thinks she's too good," basically.

I've been told by friends that I wouldn't make it out of high school. By people who basically just look at me and they don't know who I am. They only see the outer layer, so they're like, "Well, you're going to be just like the rest of them. You're going to have your first child at fifteen. You're not going to make it out of college. You're not going to make it out of high school."

I was told that I was going to be a stripper. I've been told many horrible things, but I don't let that faze me because, knowing that, I am going to work hard to make it out of that. Because I am more than that. I am more than my body. I am my body, my mind, and my soul, and I am intelligent, so that's going to take me far. Yes, sometimes it is difficult when you're doing everything positive, and then you have someone negative come in and say, "You're no better than us."

Many of the times it's people of my own ethnicity that are telling me that I won't make it out, so it's like, knowing the history, knowing that back then you didn't even have the opportunities to obtain the knowledge, and now you're having the opportunity and you're basically just pushing it to the side, that this is not necessary—it's like how can you down someone else for wanting to be successful and stable when they have the opportunities? I don't understand it.

Kaneesha has also heard the "acting white" remarks. "If I see some of my old friends from where I used to live, they'll be like, 'Why are you talking so proper and are you [acting white]?' But then when it comes to when they need help with their work and stuff like that, I say, 'So now you want my help.'"

Has ambitious Daron, who now lives with his mentors, ever been accused of "acting white"? "I hear that *now*," he says.

> I heard it this morning, as a matter of fact. It's a culmination of the people on the bus on the way here and the people where I used to live . . . The people on the bus, the people where I used to live—the lady when you get off the bus, she lives on the top of this hill. She was forever harassing me. It was, of course, my parents, all of the neighbors.
>
> There were a few select people, I would say two or three people who actually believed in what I want to accomplish. There were others who'd say, "You're trying to be white," or, as my grandmother would say, "You're trying to fit yourself in britches you can't fit."
>
> So it was hard when I first—because as a young African American male living among other African Americans who are in the same situation as I am, I felt or I hoped and expected the response to be one of great joy. However, that wasn't quite what I received. I got a lot of mixed comments, basically whether or not what I was doing was to try to belittle them and move myself up in the world. . . .

"Uppity" is the term Alonzo has heard, "a lot of times, yeah. In some families, they see you're trying to educate yourself and they take it as you're trying to be 'uppity,' that's the word they use a lot of times, or to be white, that's the term."

Andre, too, has been called "uppity" by former classmates at the public school he attended before DECA, "because they like to try to compare their homework sometimes to mine and my intellectual level to theirs, and it's not going to be even."

Geoffrey Canada, the educator known for his phenomenal successes in Harlem, recalls how he, too, had to prove himself as a bright boy growing up in the south Bronx, much as young men today still have to do. If you are a good student and live in the inner city, like the boy he calls "Scott," "Other boys are always testing you to see if you think you are better than they are. If they believe that you think so, then watch out: you become a target and might be jumped, robbed, threatened, humiliated, or ostracized. So if you're a boy like Scott, you walk a thin line. You try to be friendly and hang out with boys that provide you with social cover; the more friends you have who are known as tough kids on the block, the better your chances of not being targeted for abuse."[1] Canada explains that

> People often say to me that there seems to be a bias against poor minority children who do well in school, that they are actually punished by other kids for being "smart." This is true in many cases. The smart children are perceived as weak, and weakness is something that is often punished in poor communities. The best way I can describe it is that many children feel that their lives are so harsh, so uncertain, that when they see a child doing well in school and adopting middle-class norms and attitudes it triggers the reaction "You think I'm going to suffer and live a life of fear, fear for my future, fear for my safety, fear for my very existence, and you're gonna just waltz through life and make it out of here? No way. You ought to feel pain and fear and doubt just like the rest of us." And so they target those kids to make sure they don't escape without "paying their dues."[2]

Elijah Anderson paints a dismal picture of the urban Philadelphia area he studied:

> Since their efforts to achieve upward mobility tend to be viewed as "disrespecting" their own community, decent people, particularly children, must often struggle to advance themselves. In fact, . . . street-oriented people can often be said at times to mount a policing effort to keep their decent counterparts from "selling out" or "acting white," that is, from leaving the community for one of socioeconomic status. This retaliation, which can sometimes be violent, against the upwardly mobile points to the deep alienation present in parts of the inner-city community. Many residents therefore work to maintain the status quo, and so the individual who tries to excel usually has a great deal to overcome.[3]

Scholar Stuart Buck of the Education Reform department of the University of Arkansas reports that the "acting white" accusation is harder on boys than on girls, which might explain the lower graduation rates for boys. Quoting a Washington, D.C., journalist, he says, "A straight-arrow boy who thinks 'he's better than other people' can get taken down with violence," while "a girl of the same mien can be taken down with sex, making her a prize for a tough guy who can exhibit irresistible charms."[4]

How can this attitude exist? Haven't the nonperforming students heard about the sacrifices made by those who came before them? Don't they know that at one time it was against the law to educate a black person? Shouldn't they be grateful to those who fought the civil rights battles so that they could be educated?

Buck tells us that in 1860, only 5 percent of slaves were literate. He adds that

> Before the Civil War many states attempted to bar slaves from learning to read. For example, an 1847 Missouri law stated, "No person shall keep any school for the instruction of negroes or mulattoes, reading or writing, in this State," with a potential six-month jail term for violations. Similar laws existed across much of the South. Not just the law barred slaves from an education: slave masters often whipped, branded, cut off a finger, or even put to death slaves who had learned to read. William Henry Singleton recalls being beaten "severely" with a harness strap merely because he had been accused of briefly opening a book while carrying it for his master's son.[5]

But learn some did, in secret places like "swamps and cane-breaks," or in homes like that of a widow, a free black woman, where "we went every day about nine o'clock, with our books wrapped in paper to prevent the police or white persons from seeing them," or at secret times, as in "midnight schools," where classes were held from 11:00 or 12:00 at night until 2:00 a.m.[6]

Opposition to education for blacks continued well after the Civil War had ended, but numerous reports from northern observers exclaim over the thirst for knowledge the former slaves and their offspring exhibited: "Throughout the South, an effort is being made by the colored people to educate themselves . . . What other people on earth have ever shown, while in their ignorance, such a passion for education? . . . We have hundred—hundreds—of smart little colored children and youths, who are burning with anxiety to learn. . . . So great was the desire for instruction on the part of the blacks, that [the] teachers were often compelled to resume their task in the evening, after the labors of the day were over." [7]

This enthusiasm for education was not welcomed by many whites throughout the South, who "were very nervous about the possibility that educated blacks would start to become politically powerful," or at best, be dissatisfied with their condition in life.[8] One common saying was, "When you educate a Negro, you spoil a field hand."[9]

Nor were there many schools available for African American children who hoped to go past the eighth grade. It must have been in the 1930s that my aunt Esther, my mother's sister who taught at the white school in their small town in Kentucky, wanted more for the bright black student she had been tutoring privately. She approached my paternal grandfather, who was on the school board, to ask if there couldn't be some way that young Samuel, who had so much to offer, could join the other students at the white high school.

She was turned down; the boy would only cease to be content with his lot in life, she was told, and possibly cause trouble. (And both sides of my family were considered remarkably fair-minded for the times. As a road contractor in the South, my father insisted on the unheard-of practice of paying the black workers the same as the white ones.)

So what went wrong? How can African American young people turn their backs on what was so long denied to their forefathers?

Thomas Sowell would argue that white "rednecks," with whom black Southerners had much in common, influenced the anti-intellectualism reflected in the "acting white" slur today: "The neglect and disdain of education found among antebellum white Southerners has been echoed not only in low level performance among ghetto blacks but perhaps most dramatically in a hostility toward those black students who are conscientious about their studies, who are accused of 'acting white'—a charge that can bring anything from social ostracism to outright violence."[10]

According to Ruby K. Payne, one of the "hidden rules of poverty" for the poor of all races is that education is "valued and revered as abstract but not as reality," even though it is the key to escaping that poverty.[11]

Perhaps the roots of the "acting white" epithet can be traced back to slavery days, when household servants, usually lighter-skinned than other slaves due to their partly white ancestry, held themselves in high esteem compared with their fellow field-hand slaves.[12]

Or it could have arisen in 1892 when the case of *Plessy v. Ferguson* set into law Jim Crow customs that forbade African Americans from spaces designated for whites, but lighter skinned blacks could "act white" and pass for Caucasian. "After the Supreme Court's decision . . . those who could 'pass' as white were faced with a brutal dilemma—the American dream could be yours . . . All you have to do is deny your core being. As such, 'acting white' became synonymous with betrayal."[13]

The attitude certainly existed when W. E. B. Du Bois argued that his fellow educator Booker T. Washington, who favored "an agrarian-industrial curriculum"[14] and would not seek civil and political rights,[15] was toadying to his "wealthy white benefactors who believed in the subservience and obedience of blacks at the turn of the twentieth century in America. In their view, blacks acting as whites were socially and morally repugnant."[16]

It was Washington's "belief that blacks should receive an industrial rather than a comprehensive and well-rounded education."[17] We can argue that perhaps Washington was being practical in seeking immediate and visible rewards for his students.

W. E. B. Du Bois, the first African American to receive a Harvard doctorate, had a different vision. He and his followers believed that "blacks would gain intellectual, economic and political powers by demanding to be treated as equals of whites," as he proclaimed in his book *The Souls of Black Folk*.[18]

It was a message that the media did not welcome. "Du Bois's efforts were summarily dismissed as those of a black man seeking to act white rather than seen as those of a man pursuing an effort to transform the dream of blacks to act as equal and free participants in American society into reality"[19]—and education would pave the way.[20]

Nor was the message welcomed by the fiery Jamaica-born Marcus Garvey, who called for the self-segregation and unity of all blacks and their return to Africa to escape the damages inflicted by whites.[21] Garvey insinuated that "blacks would never be as good as or equal to whites."[22] He believed that "blacks receiving a formal education were serving as lackeys of whites—in essence, acting white,"[23] and, to Garvey, Du Bois was the greatest lackey of all.

In contrast, and fortunately for the future of the country, "The early efforts of W. E. B. Du Bois and the NAACP [which he helped to found] had a more lasting impact on American culture—in particular the belief that blacks who seek to become equal participants in American society, armed with the knowledge gained through education, were acting responsibly."[24]

And yet the "acting white" insult was carried forward. Even the civil rights leaders of the 1960s were accused. "In the eyes of Malcolm X," says Ron Christie, Martin Luther King Jr. "was nothing more than an Uncle Tom acting white by trying to achieve societal change by working with whites."[25]

Barack Obama has also been the target of the slur. Following a racial incident in Louisiana in which six black students were punished for attacking a white student—unfairly, according to Jesse Jackson—the reverend accused the then-senator of "acting like he's white" for failing to bring more attention to the case.[26]

"America has long had a strain of anti-intellectualism—both among blacks and whites," Buck says. "But something happened in the 1960s that made some black children start to believe that education was *for white people, not for them.*"[27] The antiestablishment attitudes of the turbulent 1960s were applied to education, as well.

"For blacks," says Columbia's John McWhorter, "the idea that one's value as a black American was one's difference from whites . . . fit right in with a new black identity based too often on being in opposition to The Man." Attitudes toward education became yet another manifestation of this opposition.[28]

The "acting white" phenomenon, he claims, is a "particularly clear manifestation" of the "therapeutic alienation" of the late 1960s, when not succeeding in school was a way of "setting oneself off against an oppressor," and as a "badge of racial identity."[29] He notes that it was only then that the performance gap began. It was no coincidence that it was accompanied by the "acting white" judgment when black children began to attend desegregated schools.

As Buck says, with integration, "The safe and sheltering environment of black schools—once the center of the black community—disappeared. In their place was the integrated school, which was more unfriendly to black students, and less likely to feature black role models of academic success. As a result, black students became alienated from the world of school. They began to think of the school as a 'white' institution,"[30] especially when the majority of teachers were white.[31]

"Even though many segregated black schools were doing the best that they could," says Buck, "they were not fully able to overcome centuries of slavery, oppression, and economic hardship."[32] After attending such substandard schools, many were placed in classes for slow learners; if you wanted to be loyal to your group, you'd aim no higher. Harvard's Roland Fryer Jr. "found that the 'acting white' criticism is unique to integrated schools, while in predominantly black schools, there is '*no evidence at all* that getting good grades adversely affects students' popularity.'"[33]

It was in the civil rights period of the 1960s that O. Lewis used the notion of "oppositional disposition" in order to explain the failed academic performance of poor minority students. The term expressed the "belief that school failure reflected 'both an adaptation and a reaction of the poor to their marginal position in a class-stratified, highly individuated, capitalistic society.'"[34]

The anthropologist John Ogbu agreed that African American students have done less well than they could "in order not to be seen by their African American peers as standing apart from their identity,"[35] while S. Fordham suggested that "minority students do not succeed academically because for them success in school is equated with 'acting white.'"[36]

Not only can the fear of "acting white" affect grades; it can also "deter blacks from participating in the very activities or classes that go along with academic success," says Buck.[37]

It is human nature to want to be part of a group; we're more comfortable with people like ourselves. Sociologists note, however, that the African American culture rates much higher on group importance that does the Euro-American, mainstream culture. As a "high-context" group, it's a more homogenous society in which much is understood without the need for words. On the high-context/low-context scale of fifteen cultures, Edward T. Hall would place the African American fourth from the top (Japan being at the top), while the North American culture in general is fourth from the bottom.[38]

So although harassment of "nerds" is nothing new,[39] the peer pressure must be even stronger among African American young people than among their white contemporaries. It's also painful to set yourself apart from family, especially when the family resents this separation. As Payne notes, "to move from poverty . . . , an individual must give up relationships for achievement, (at least for some period of time)."[40]

Thomas Sowell asserts that "groupthink" is not always a good thing, for it "does not always lead to wiser decisions than what emerges from a clash of differing individual ideas from within the group. Most dangerously, group solidarity often means letting the lowest common denominator shape the culture and life within the group and determine the direction of its future."

He gives as an example "black students being accused of 'acting white' for being conscientious about their studies."[41]

Consider, too, how education requires long-term commitment, not the instant gratification preached by the hip-hop "artists." As one critic noted in *The Atlantic Monthly*, the message of rap is that "parents nurturing children and believing in education as a long-term investment is . . . for suckers."[42]

The anthropologist John Ogbu named another reason for the achievement gap: the "black folk theories of effort and reward," according to which "hard work does not pay."[43] It did not seem worth making the effort if there were no jobs out there anyway. "Because black students expect that they will face discrimination in the labor market at some future point, they have little reason to value education," Buck agrees.[44]

Given all the "potholes," as Jewel would put it, that get in the way of DECA students pursuing their dreams of a higher education, their strength— or perhaps their good sense—in overcoming the "acting white" epithet is remarkable. Jewanna talks about those who drop out of school:

> That's the one sad thing to me, because it's like people say, "I need this. I need that. Everything is chaotic. This is happening at home. That's happening at home. So I'm not going to school." How is that solving your problem? Why do you think not going to school is going to help you get out of that situation? That makes me so mad. You need your education! If you don't come to school, if you can't get out of your situation, you're going to be in the same situation you're in now. You don't have any kind of sense when you think like that.

Jewel, now in college, remembers being called "lame," which is the opposite of "cool":

> I had friends that were doing what you shouldn't be doing, negative things. Well, because I was in DECA—students typically call it "lame," but because I was willing to, you know, be an outsider or be an oddball and just really submerge myself in it and take full advantage of DECA, it allowed me to almost bypass some of those potholes.
>
> I mean, even in my own family I see some of my own generation not going to school or not going to college, not finishing high school. If you don't do what the norm is, or if you're not in like the cool group of students, somebody who's popular, they will call you "lame." That's their way of saying that you're not popular, you're not with it, like you need to keep up.

"We got that all the time," Vanetta agrees, and Jewel continues:

> Even when we would go downtown and catch the bus, they would be like, "There are those DECA kids." They would come and just mess with us, and say, "You all think you're all so smart." We really had to experience things like that just because people thought we were lame, and we thought we were smart.

How did they handle it? "A lot of times you have to ignore it," says Vanetta, "a lot of times you just had to come and take the higher road . . . You just had to kind of understand the culture for it. For Jewel and me, we come from the inner-city environment and we also come from abusive households. Jewel, her family was more toward the physical abusive side, and mine was more toward the verbal abusive side. So we kind of got the profit, I'm going to call it, of how things can play out, if that makes sense."

Although DECA students claim that they are no more intelligent than most young people their age, they possess a special strength, like Alonzo, who lived alone at the age of twelve when his mother left him at home when she went south to care for an ailing relative.

Alonzo explains how fear of exclusion can keep some people from leaving the familiar:

> Some people do not know anything outside of Dayton. The athletes I've seen, the best athletes do not want to leave the city, even though there are good opportunities such as go to college, play college basketball, but some of them just do not want to leave. I don't know—well, I do know. It's the fact that they haven't had exposure, they haven't had an individual counseling them, telling them it's OK to leave, do what you have to do.
>
> Whether from their household, family, friend, [there hasn't been anyone] to actually express to them that it's fine to leave and go and come back. You won't be looked at any differently. I think a lot of times, too, people leave and then they come back and people who are not where they're at, people who stayed here and are not as successful, they have a tendency to put down a person who left to try to better themselves, and I think that fear of not being accepted by their environment if they come back is the reason also why they don't want to leave.

But Alonzo has never gotten the "acting white" slur, because, he explains, "I think people understand me, where I come from, and I know who I am. I never try to be something I'm not. I grew up in [the inner city], I go to college, I'm a graduate of DECA, I never try to be somebody I wasn't. Ask anybody, I always stuck tight to my morals and different things I believed, and never wavered."

I asked him why it is so hard for other people. Don't they have his self-confidence? He replied:

> I ask myself this all the time. Sometimes I sit up and talk to [my former advisor] Mrs. Jones, and I really reach the point where I want to cry. I'm like, what makes me so different? Why did I make it and my friend right here didn't make it, or why did I make it, and he kind of made it, but I'm at the point where I'm ahead, and he's not. . . . Sometimes I don't really understand what makes me different, but at the same time I know I've been given the opportunity to do something special, so I'm taking it and running with it.

I really do think that the decisions you make today affect you four or five years from now. And I think one key difference for me, and I think it's a problem for a lot of people, is that I had people around me that were there, people who were very influential, who were good influences.

As an individual, I was very open-minded, I always believed in listening. I'm a great listener. I'd rather not talk, I'd rather listen from time to time. What I do is observe, then I'm able to give my unbiased opinion about different things. And then the fact that when I was young, I was kind of strong-minded, I had good people around me, and that combination really made me different. I didn't make the mistakes that other people made. I listened to Mrs. Jones, to Dr. Hennessey.

Dannisha, who proudly sits up tall and straight, has a great deal of confidence in her own abilities. For her, the question of peer pressure not to succeed is overrated, "because," she says, "you find in any environment groups of people who are for you and groups of people who are against you. So I think that to focus on—well, let's call it what it is—the ghetto—OK, this is not the only place where you'll ever find that, when it's a really common thing."

"You know, when you go into a workplace, you don't always find people who are supportive of your goals. No one's going to ask you, 'Hey, how's your promotion going?' So I don't think that it's a thing that's really common, but I will say you can find people who are supportive and people who are not supportive in any environment." It is the determination to escape poverty that motivates this top-ranking senior to succeed.

Leaving old friends behind may be a painful part of growing up and away as DECA students go down a different road. The time and effort that DECA requires can be a real roadblock to maintaining old friendships.

"Before I came to DECA," Vanetta says, "I had a big group of friends. Like I said, that was before I came, but after I got here I ended pretty much with Jewel, right here! Just because it requires a lot of your time, and if you're not here to experience DECA, you will have a totally different outlook and people will think that you're distancing them and you no longer want to hang out with them, but really it's because DECA raises the bar and so you're going to have to step up to it or you will fall behind.

"And so I did really change. I didn't change in a bad way; I didn't change who I was, but like I said, it calls you to a high level of excellence." In fact, at DECA, says freshman Sabrana, there's a different kind of peer pressure: "If you're failing and you're mean to the teachers, people don't like you . . . The people who are failing that have been in their freshman class since their freshman year and they [should be] juniors now, they're not cool."

NOTES

1. Geoffrey Canada, *Reaching Up for Manhood: Transforming the Lives of Boys in America* (Boston: Beacon Press, 1998), 90.

2. Geoffrey Canada, *Fist, Stick, Knife, Gun: A Personal Story of Violence* (Boston: Beacon Press, 1995), 153–54.

3. Elijah Anderson, *Code of the Street: Decency, Violence, and the Moral Life of the Inner City* (New York: Norton, 1999), 65.

4. Stuart Buck, *Acting White: The Ironic Legacy of Desegregation* (New Haven, CT: Yale University Press, 2010), 15.

5. Buck, *Acting White*, 43.

6. Buck, *Acting White*, 44.

7. Buck, *Acting White*, 46–48.

8. Buck, *Acting White*, 47.

9. Buck, *Acting White*, 46.

10. Thomas Sowell, *Black Rednecks and White Liberals* (San Francisco: Encounter Books, 2005), 30.

11. Ruby K. Payne, *A Framework for Understanding Poverty*, 4th rev. ed. (Highlands, TX: AHA! Process, Inc., 2005), 42.

12. Sowell, *Black Rednecks and White Liberals*, 42–43.

13. Ron Christie, *Acting White: The Curious History of a Racial Slur* (New York: Thomas Dunn/St. Martin's Press, 2010), 51.

14. Christie, *Acting White*, 52.

15. Christie, *Acting White*, 32.

16. Christie, *Acting White*, 52.

17. Christie, *Acting White*, 32.

18. Christie, *Acting White*, 52.

19. Christie, *Acting White*, 65.

20. Christie, *Acting White*, 66.

21. Christie, *Acting White*, 72.

22. Christie, *Acting White*, 86.

23. Christie, *Acting White*, 86.

24. Christie, *Acting White*, 87.

25. Christie, *Acting White*, 109.

26. Christie, *Acting White*, 197.

27. Buck, *Acting White*, 141.

28. John McWhorter, *Winning the Race: Beyond the Crisis in Black America* (New York: Gotham/Penguin, 2006), 141.

29. McWhorter, *Winning the Race*, 261.

30. Buck, *Acting White*, 74.

31. Buck, *Acting White*, 76.

32. Buck, *Acting White*, 116.

33. Quoted in Buck, *Acting White*, 11.

34. Marvin Lynn, A. Dee Williams, Grace Benigno, Colleen Mitchell, and Gloria Park, "Race, Class, and Gender in Urban Education," in Joe L. Kincheloe, kecia hayes, Karel Rose, and Philip M. Anderson, eds., *Urban Education*, 89–101 (Lanham, MD: Rowman & Littlefield, 2007), 91.

35. Rod Paige and Elaine Witty, *The Black-White Achievement Gap: Why Closing It Is the Greatest Civil Rights Issue of Our Time* (New York: American Management Association, 2010), 66.

36. Lynn et al., "Race, Class, and Gender in Urban Education," 91.

37. Buck, *Acting White*, 17.

38. Larry A. Samovar, Richard E. Porter, and Edwin R. McDaniel, *Communication between Cultures*, 7th ed. (Belmont, CA: Thomson/Wadsworth, 2010), 216.

39. Julie Landsman, *A White Teacher Talks About Race* (Lanham, MD: Scarecrow Press, 2001), 43–44

40. Payne, *A Framework for Understanding Poverty*, 11.

41. Sowell, *Black Rednecks and White Liberals*, 284.

42. Juan Williams, *Enough: The Phony Leaders, Dead-End Movements, and Culture of Failure That Are Undermining Black America—And What We Can Do About It* (New York: Three Rivers Press, 2006), 141.

43. Paige and Witty, *The Black-White Achievement Gap*, 66.

44. Buck, *Acting White*, 142.

Chapter Five

Inadequate Schools

Drugs, violence, chaotic home situations, poverty, peer pressure—but there's one more challenge DECA students have had to overcome. The quality of the schools they have attended before DECA have left them far behind those with whom they'll have to compete in college.

"The average black high school senior in America," says Stuart Buck, "is performing at about the level of white eighth graders," and "the average black student's SAT score in 2006 was 200 points lower than the average white student's score."[1] [2] African Americans who have gotten good grades in high school are stunned when they fail courses in college.[3]

Kanika Jones, teacher/coach at DECA, describes the "culture shock" that new students might experience when they enter DECA:

> We have some battles with students who know other students who've gone here and think, "I'm just as smart," and then they get here and they realize they have to work, because a lot of students that we get have a preconceived notion that "Oh, I was smart. I got all A's. I was the best in my class."
>
> Depending on where they went to school, being quiet and sitting in their seats, not necessarily doing the work, could have probably granted them an A, or they could have been given work that they completed on time and they were given an A, but it doesn't necessarily mean that it was on grade level.

The film and book *Waiting for "Superman"* dramatically brought our attention to the low quality of schools throughout America. We learned how bad teachers with union-guaranteed tenure, immune from dismissal, are shuffled from one school to another in what's called "the dance of the lemons," and of the infamous "rubber rooms," which have since been closed, "where suspended teachers wait for a hearing, often kept on salary for years, doing nothing."[4]

And we learned that when Michelle Rhee, then-chancellor of the District of Columbia school system, proposed a merit-based salary that would almost double current salaries in exchange for the loss of tenure, the union refused to consider the matter, choosing security over pay.

Although Harlem educator Geoffrey Canada believes that the unions "have done a good job of representing educators as employees and defending their rights," he also thinks that

> Teacher contracts define with excessive specificity what a teacher can and cannot do in a classroom. And once you define everything that can happen in a school—how many hours teachers work, how many classes they teach, how long their lunch breaks and bathroom breaks are, and the details of their compensation structures—you deprive the leader, the principal, the director, and even the teachers themselves of the ability to try new things, thereby strangling any hope of innovation. . . . Consider, for example, the simple matter of hours in the school day and days in the school year. If a child is two years behind in reading and math, shouldn't he or she get the opportunity to stay in school for a longer day to catch up with the other students?

After all, he argues, "In most rationally run businesses, employees have to work late when they fall behind, but you can't do that in public education."[5]

Public schools also suffer from a top-heavy bureaucracy that can stifle teacher initiative. As Abigail and Stephan Thernstrom assert, "Big-city superintendents and principals operate in a bureaucratic and political strait-jacket. Indeed, the very nature of their jobs encourages inertia. Doing a good job, doing what's necessary to get ahead, requires playing by the rules and staying out of trouble. Even the best superintendents say they have to work around the system to get the job done."[6]

It's one more thing to lay at the unions' doorstep, with their "rigid rules and regulations." They conclude that "without incentives for excellence and innovation, and the discretionary power to meet the needs of students, no wonder so many schools are so disappointing."[7]

It is the overpowering bureaucracy of public schools that has led many to consider that charter schools are better able to meet students' needs. "Under most existing bureaucracies," charter supporters believe, "true innovation and independence are impossible and that this tyranny can be blamed for at least part of the current crisis in education"; Peter Cookson and Kristina Berger report that the excessive paperwork required by such a system "prevents teachers from creating new lesson plans. The archaic structure of the daily schedule at most public schools prevents collaboration and cross-fertilization among teachers—and between teachers at different schools. Meddling school leadership . . . creates an environment in which teachers are discouraged from spending extra time at school or participating on after-hours school leadership teams. District-wide initiatives that require schools to use a single set of textbooks and approved curricula remove local control over what is taught from teachers and parents."[8] [9]

As the community activist Bill Strickland states in *Waiting for "Superman,"* we need to loosen "the stranglehold of traditional bureaucratic, political, and union rules" if we are to improve our schools.[10] It's an opinion shared by the education reformers Steven Zemelman, Harvey Daniels, and Arthur Hyde, who point out that there have been too many standards. Thus teachers have been "told by their states what to teach, when to teach it, and how—often in pre-scripted word-for-word, 'teacher-proof' programs that not only [have ruled out] teachers' creativity, but their humanity as well."[11]

The centenarian and veteran teacher Evangeline Lindsley would certainly concur. As she used to say, "Teaching is a profession. To me the teacher in the classroom is like a surgeon in the operating room. You've got to rely on the teacher who touches the child, and [the state's] policies don't seem to do that. The teacher in the classroom is the one who knows what has to be done. The teacher knows the child." She looked back to better days when there were only a handful of administrators.[12]

Administrators have had their hands tied, too, according to Abigail Thernstrom and Stephan Thernstrom, for principals have "little control over their staff, resources, or discipline policy."[13] Nor do superintendents enjoy autonomy either.[14] Instead, they claim, quoting political scientist Terry M. Moe, "Unions 'are the preeminent power in American education.'"[15]

The fifteen thousand students in the Dayton Public Schools, where close to 80 percent of the students qualify for free or reduced-price lunches,[16] apparently fare no better than those in other poor districts.

"When Ohio issued its first district and school-level report cards in 1998," say Chester Finn, Terry Ryan, and Michael Lafferty, "they confirmed what most Daytonians had known for at least a decade: the Gem City's public schools were in academic tatters." As the *Cleveland Plain Dealer* reported, "With dwindling enrollments and abysmal test scores, the [Dayton] school district looked like a poster child for all that was wrong with the big urban school systems. Too many students were dropping out. Too many never came at all. There was little or no discipline. Teacher morale sagged. School board members bickered. Deficits soared."[17]

In a Harvard-sponsored study in 2004, DECA students "underscore[d] their previous educational experiences of minimal challenge and sub-level coursework in chaotic classrooms. Students often depicted their teachers in previous schools as struggling to get through the day." There is no attempt at motivation, said one student. "You really don't see that the teachers care. . . . They just want to get their paycheck. If they get it, it's fine. They really don't try to encourage the kids to go further into their education."[18] In spite of the call for reform, not much has changed in the intervening years.

One roadblock to raising teacher performance, says Dr. Thomas Lasley, former dean of education at the University of Dayton, may be that, unlike in other professions, "there's no agreement as to a defined set of skills that a teacher should possess when they [leave college], so the skills that you learn as a teacher are going to vary to a certain extent, based on where you went to school." He cites a lack of conformity in methods of assessments and, referring to numerous discipline problems in Texas schools, he notes that

> If you look at all the ways in which teachers are prepared, depending on whether they went to the University of Houston or North Texas State, or wherever you went, you may have gotten a very different set of strategies for dealing with discipline. There's no common way to share that knowledge with pre-service teachers. If you go to law school and you learn about torts, actually because of the bar, as a law student you basically are going to learn [the same thing]. It's about the same content whether you go to Ohio State or Capital University.
>
> Deborah Ball at the University of Michigan has said the reason that teacher preparation is in such crisis . . . is because we have not been able to do what most professions have been able to do, and that is narrow the skills that we need to deliver to pre-service teachers so that they all enter with parallel sets of skills and to make sure they really know those skills and how to use them.

Kalman R. Hettleman is more outspoken. The Baltimore politician, former school board member, and education-policy analyst cites the "overwhelming evidence that undergraduate and graduate teacher-education programs are deficient even at teaching teachers to teach," let alone producing quality managers.[19]

DECA students are well aware of what they had been missing. Jewel looks at her experience coming from a public school to DECA: "I believe when I came in, coming from other Dayton public schools, I had what I like to think of as potholes in my education foundation [that had to be filled in]. I think it's kind of like if you build a house on a badly built foundation or a broken foundation, the house eventually will kind of crumble to pieces."

The education she received at the school she attended earlier "was actually horrible at the time," she says:

> My social studies teacher would have us stack the books up on the floor, we put all the books on top of each other. She talked on the phone the whole class, and the rule was you come in class, you pick up a book when you walk in, and you read the chapter and do the chapter review in the back. And so while she would just sit there and talk to her friends on the phone, we would just be sitting there reading the chapter and doing the chapter review in the back. And when you leave, you put the paper that you wrote on her desk and stack the books back up. The next group of kids that come in, they do the same thing.
>
> You don't learn like that. For one, sometimes I'd find myself not even reading, and I would just look at the questions and try and look for the answer.

If they're not really engaging you, you're not really learning. You know it's not sticking with you. It's just kind of going in one ear and out the other. . . .

I think people just kind of—it's a job for them, like "I don't care whether you learn or not. I'm going to get paid." And when people have that mentality . . . if it's just a paycheck for you, that's when those potholes and those issues come into the students' education, because when you're young, as a child all the way up, those are the most important times in your life, anyway.

You know, children are like sponges and they soak up every bit of knowledge that you teach them. So if you damage that period of time or don't take full advantage of it, then they will be behind. They can turn out to be successful, but it will be a lot harder and they'll have to do a lot of work.

In my math classes the students drove the teachers all crazy, and my math teacher quit. And they actually—they didn't get us a sub, they sent like the security down to our class. I mean, this is a real story! They sent a security man down for our class, to just kind of watch and supervise our class. And that's it.

Although violent crimes are rare in our nation's public schools, according to Thernstrom and Thernstrom, there is plenty of "plain disorder, incivility, and disobedience. . . . Beepers going off, provocative clothing, desks turned over, yammering, singing, rude remarks to teachers, marijuana sold in bathrooms. . . . Undercover police and metal detectors most often keep guns and knives out of school, but such measures do not stop everyday chaos."[20]

Nor are the guards and detectors always successful. Providing a safe school environment is one thing Dannisha would change in the public schools: "One of my cousins went to [a public high school]—and he was able to bring a gun to school, and they have security guards, and a metal detector. How did he get that in there? It was not that difficult. Somebody was not doing their job, so hire people who are qualified, that are not afraid to do what they need to do when they need to do it, because it needs to be done."

At Vanetta's middle school, she says,

I felt like I was dumb or I was stupid, and college was just for smart people. I had bad teachers. I had some good teachers, but I had some bad teachers. I had teachers say that we wouldn't make it. I would have teachers treat me different because it took me longer to learn something. I actually had a teacher tell me I wasn't going to be able to get by on my looks. My middle-school experience was probably much like Jewel's, because to be honest, a lot of my peer group are in jail. . . .

I would say for many young people, especially for many inner-city young people, there is the expectation that you're not going to succeed, whether it's in the environment or in the educational system. And it's just reinforced once you go into the schools. If you have a destructive home life, or you have someone who is verbally abusive or physically abusive and you don't have those resources to get help, or to even have the resources to speak about it, it ultimately can lead you down a self-destructive path.

In addition to suffering from all the problems associated with being poor, inner-city African American students are victims of what George W. Bush called "the soft bigotry of low expectations."[21] In fact, Ron Christie asserts that "the allegation of acting white is nothing more than the perpetuation" of this bigoted belief that blacks are incapable of intellectual achievement, which has been "accepted by our society by blacks and whites for too long."[22] Insisting on hard work and "raising the bar of expectations" for black students, he says, "will be a difficult and painful process that must be undertaken to establish a benchmark and a baseline for success."[23]

Psychologist and educator Kenneth Clark "believes that a key component of the deprivation that afflicts ghetto children is that generally their teachers do not expect them to learn; the teachers think of their function as being one simply of custodial care and discipline."[24]

How would DECA students change the system? "Have teachers that are not afraid to motivate students, inspire students, and expect the best," says Dannisha, "not something like, 'OK, you're going to get a mediocre job, you're going to get a marginal job.' No, expect the best out of their students."

Parents, as well as their children, are well aware of the deficiencies at other schools. Sabrana's mother felt her daughter lacked challenge at the Catholic school she attended before. When she entered DECA in the seventh grade, she was reading at a fifth-grade level, even though she was getting straight A's on her report card. Now, however, the freshman student is reading at the eleventh-grade level. And fellow student LaTonya says:

> My mother told me, "If you don't get into DECA, you're not going to Dayton Public Schools. You need to go to a school that is very competitive. If I have to send you away, I'm going to send you away." And I told her, "If you have to send me away, *please* send me away, because they want to send me to [a public high school]" and I wasn't going to go there, because that school would not push me, and that's not the type of environment that I want to be in.
>
> I have friends who go to the public school, and they basically don't care, because they feel like the teachers are just there for a paycheck. So instead of actually putting that passion into what you are teaching, you are basically just giving them [nothing], because at the end of the day or the week you're still going to get that paycheck. I guess it's that negativity in the school which then makes the teachers not care, because they're in that negative environment.
>
> I think it's basically a recurring cycle. It's the teachers, but it's also the students . . . I don't think I would have made it in the public schools in Dayton, personally. I would have lost my sanity.

Robert tries to describe the difference in what's expected at the public schools and DECA. At the public school, "they had expectations but it was more standard, like going through the motions. DECA has the expectation, and DECA meets the expectation. DPS [Dayton Public Schools] probably has had the same expectation for years, and you really don't see a change in

meeting that expectation, or even improvement. DPS may set an expectation . . . but they don't have the necessary programs, teachers, people, time,
to reach that expectation."

He laughs as he tries to find an analogy: "So their expectation is more like
an expectation that's just floating in the air, as opposed to our expectation.
Our expectation, it floats, but we go get it. It's floating up in the air, but we
go get it. We make sure we go grab that expectation! It's never out of our
reach. We just go get a ladder, climb and we get it!"

Charter schools, while touted by some as a cure-all for the problems of
public education, do not always measure up, either.

"I went to the Academy of Dayton," says Daron, who hopes to go into
politics. "There I wasn't as challenged as much as I would like to have been.
I've always been a charmer. I was able to talk my way through a lot of
different things . . . sort of talking myself out of situations rather than actually
do the work. However, when I did work, I wasn't challenged enough, and I
honestly think that's what led me to having those issues [of not doing well].
If I didn't feel like it was hard enough, I really didn't want to do it."

Marcus, now a sophomore at an Ivy League college, recalls that at the
charter school he attended in middle school, "one teacher talked about her
new shoes rather than concentrating on the lesson."

Shawna, looking back on her middle-school years, draws a blank, she
says. "I mean, I didn't learn anything, really. The teachers had no problem
telling us that 'you are eighth-graders being taught from a sixth-grade book.'
That really angered me, because I felt that there were not any standards—the
standards were well below our grade level. I always knew that I wanted to go
to college, but then I thought at the end of my eighth-grade year, 'Am I
prepared for high school, let alone college?'"

At the Catholic school that Dannisha had attended, due to the fact that "a
lot of low-income students had just come out of public schools that had been
closed," she says, "a lot of the kids that ended up attending the school were
coming from the same background as me, so you really found the same
public-school atmosphere: a lot of the kids weren't studying, so we were
spending time going over the same thing over and over and over again, and
so it got very repetitive. It was really monotonous, and I was like, 'OK, let's
start this over.'"

There is no comparison between his present school and the middle school
he attended before, says Demarco. There, "I really didn't have to do anything
to pass, so it was just like sitting back and relaxing in class for the most part.
Coming to DECA, it really challenged me to work and use my mind. So I'm
thankful for that."

Compared to DECA, where "the expectations are different," Jolena
agrees that "at Dayton Public you're not expected to go above and beyond. . . . You're expected to graduate high school and get your diploma. At

DECA you're expected to graduate, get the diploma, and go on to college and then after college become great in your career, which is not a main goal at Dayton Public."

Not expecting enough from the students in America's low-income districts is a complaint the experts frequently raise and one echoed by Teach for America, which recruits and trains recent college graduates for two-year teaching assignments in low-income areas.[25] According to a 2005 survey of its corps members,

> Expectations of students—from teachers, schools, parents, the general public, and students themselves—are both a powerful tool and a powerful obstacle. Corps members see low expectations as a significant cause in the achievement gap. They believe that expanding a common belief in the potential of low-income students and students of color is key to closing the gap. Indeed, their experience as teachers has strengthened their belief in their students' belief to meet high expectations.[26]

Julie Landsman, a white teacher in a school for troubled teens, wondered if white teachers have unconsciously expected less from their black students.[27] She also suggests that perhaps white teachers, especially, might be afraid to discipline students or to expect more from them, even though the black teachers who were strict were appreciated: "It shows they respect us. . . . Shows they *expect* us to behave," said one student.[28]

Award-winning educator Lisa Delpit quotes a twelve-year-old African American friend who divides the teachers at his middle school into three groups: "the black teachers, none of whom are afraid of black kids; the white teachers, a few of whom are not afraid of black kids; and the largest group of white teachers, who are *all* afraid of black kids,"[29] with the intrinsic discipline problems of the third group.

Delpit claims that different styles involved in communication might be at the root of some of the problems. While African American teachers are more apt to use direct commands, like "Put your books away now!", white teachers are inclined to use a softer, indirect form: "Would you like to put your books away now?" The former style conveys a sense of power that commands respect, while the latter indicates weakness and a lack of power to which the students respond negatively.[30]

In an integrated Chicago suburban school, reports David Shipler, the "virtually all-white faculty" confessed that they were uneasy about confronting black males who misbehaved, and African American males, who made up a disproportionate number of disciplinary cases, were punished more severely than whites.

The same apprehension among white teachers existed in the New Jersey high school that Shipler examined, where white teachers "'feel they don't want to discipline the kids, because they're afraid they're going to be insulted.' . . . Some teachers feel caught in the middle, damned whichever way they go. 'If I come down too tough or too hard on my kids, then I'm being a mean SOB,' complained a middle-aged white woman. 'If I act too understanding, I'm "enabling,"' meaning that she was enabling blacks to drift along on an undisciplined, unchallenged path that would never get them ahead."[31] Class, rather than race, is also an issue, as James Deneen and Carm Catanese point out: "The behavioral norms of many students from impoverished neighborhoods may differ greatly from those of their teachers, many of whom come from a middle-class socioeconomic background."[32]

Although "race issues can certainly be present," class differences are important, too: "Because teachers are just about 100 percent middle-class, while many of their inner-city charges are poor, considerable friction and misunderstanding occur," and "the cultural gap between teachers and students . . . can grow to unfortunate proportions," say Zemelman, Daniels, and Hyde. Misunderstanding can lead to the "heartbreaking . . . amount of anger and hostility we see in urban schools. The kids can seem wild, and the teachers yell and label them harshly to their faces to maintain basic control."[33]

Even though Jolena liked her public school teachers, it was difficult for them to do their job, because "they had so many students they had to worry about, and there was so much stress about kids fighting, home things, you know. There were home things that were challenging and causing more problems at school. And the classrooms were much bigger, so the teachers didn't have as much time to focus on the students individually."

In the face of chaos, schools might resort to functioning in the authoritarian, no nonsense—and no fun—way like those described in Jonathan Kozol's bestseller *The Shame of the Nation*. Inner-city schools "that have embraced a pedagogy of direct command and absolute control" use the approaches of B. F. Skinner "commonly employed in penal institutions and drug-rehabilitation programs."[34]

Can white teachers understand the culture from which their poor black students come? There are real cultural differences between the African American subculture and mainstream European-influenced culture, says Edward T. Hall, who found differences of body language, eye contact, and personal space between whites and blacks. Hall even claimed that "such unconscious differences may well be one of the sources of what blacks feel is the basic racism of white society."[35]

Bryson, a DECA senior, notes that in the public schools, "the average teacher is Caucasian female, and it's kind of like a mismatch between the background of the students."

Bryson, like so many of his classmates, has given a lot of thought to what we need to do to get America going:

You know, the first thing on my mind is basically if we want the country to improve, we have to start with education, and most of our students who go to school attend school in these urban areas, so we need to figure out ways to fix that, the school problems that are going on in these areas.

I mentioned the break between the backgrounds of the teachers and the students, ineffective teachers, teachers who know the material but who aren't able to cope with the background, or unable to cope with the environment to be effective in their teaching. A lot of the students don't have the materials that they need. We don't have the technology a lot of the times, the books that we need, to compete with these other students.

There are not a lot of things going on to help with them with their home life, to help them do better with school. There's a whole slew of issues going on in the urban areas that we need to correct if we want these students to be able to compete with students in the suburban areas, who from birth are taught the networking and are introduced to all these things that they need to be successful. How can we expect [urban students] to be successful if they're not given the tools or the attention that they need?

Like the anthropologist Edward T. Hall, Gloria Ladson-Billings calls our attention to the African-based sense of the group among American blacks. She quotes teacher Patricia Hilliard: "The African world view suggests that 'I am because *we* are, and because *we* are. I am. . . . One's self-identity is therefore always a *people* identity."[36]

Hall, who places African American culture high on the scale of high-context cultures, has more to say about groups in general: The ideal size for a "working group," he says, is between eight and twelve individuals. This is natural, because man evolved as a primate while living in small groups.

"There are also a variety of compelling reasons why this particular size range is the most productive and efficient. Eight to twelve persons can know each other well enough to maximize their talents. In groups beyond this size the possible combinations of communication between individuals get too complex to handle; people are lumped into categories and begin the process of ceasing to exist as individuals. And yet, he adds, "We consistently discriminate against all our children and young people when we subject them to massive learning situations."[37]

Is it any wonder, then, that Julie Landsman, as a teacher in a school for troubled teens, would say, "There is nothing more obvious to teachers and nothing makes me angrier than to be told that class size does not matter. . . . There is no question that small class sizes make a huge difference in our ability to reach all students."[38]

Added to the problem is "the constant churning of children between schools," that Finn, Ryan, and Lafferty have perceived in Ohio.[39] When jobs are lost, when the rent can't be paid, or when relationships break up, those in poverty move on, as in Jewel's case: "I can't even remember what schools I went to, I switched around so much. We moved around a lot, me and my brother and my mom. Every year we moved, like to a new house or a new apartment, so I never had actual school ties or school spirit, because I was always meeting a new group of kids."

We must give credit to those public-school teachers, like Jolena's, however, who recognized that some of the students they encountered deserved more than their schools could offer.

It was a counselor for anger management who saw the potential in Andre. Perhaps his frequent fights at school were a call for help. His mother, his pastor, "everybody was like, 'Yeah, you've got to go to DECA, because the Dayton Public Schools, you just flow through them with ease,'" he says. "I'm very intelligent so I catch up on things pretty easily, and I could just slack my way through high school."

Other teachers, too, took an interest in him: An eighth-grade math teacher was a great influence, as was the principal of the high school. "She helped me out also, because before then I was like a student who just got A's and B's, and she started acknowledging me more, having me coming to meetings and luncheons with her with other students, and it was kind of nice to see that. Before then, I never really had a relationship with any of my teachers. I would kind of pass the classes and keep moving on. After my middle school, that's when a lot of teachers were like, 'You have the potential to do whatever you want to do. You have the mind for it, you have the desire, and you have the push from your family, so you can do it if you want.'"

Andre regrets that his brother, who dropped out of school in the twelfth grade and has lived on the edge of the law, had no one to recognize his intelligence, to say, "You have the potential to do this." It might have made a difference, he thinks, "because my brother is real smart, like he's more of a philosopher kind of person. When he's talking, you have to have a higher order of thinking just to understand what he's saying sometimes."

Should we have any doubts about the deleterious effect of substandard schools, we can ponder what Patricia Hilliard, an experienced teacher in another urban area, has to say about the "powerful negative impact poor schooling has" on those she teaches in the inner city:

> Some of the smartest youngsters I've worked with have been right here in this community, but a lot of the time they don't believe in themselves. School saps the life out of them. You want to see intelligence walking around on two legs? Just go into a kindergarten class. They come to school with fresh faces, full of wonder. But by third grade you can see how badly school has beaten them down. You can really see it in the boys. I sometimes ask myself just what it is we're doing to these children.[40]

"Perhaps the most devastating and damaging thing that can happen to someone," warns Edward T. Hall, "is to fail to fulfill his potential. A kind of gnawing emptiness, longing, frustration, and displaced anger overwhelms people when this occurs, whether the anger is turned inward on the self, or outward toward others, dreadful destruction results."[41]

NOTES

1. Stuart Buck, *Acting White: The Ironic Legacy of Desegregation* (New Haven, CT: Yale University Press, 2010), 29.

2. The racial gap persists, according to SAT results for 2011.

3. Abigail Thernstrom and Stephan Thernstrom, *No Excuses: Closing the Racial Gap* (New York: Simon & Schuster, 2003),, 34.

4. Karl Weber, Introduction, "'Waiting for Superman'—The Story Behind the Movie," in Karl Weber, ed., *Waiting for "Superman"* (New York: Public Affairs/Perseus, 2010), 20.

5. Geoffrey Canada, "Bringing Change to Scale: The Next Big Reform Challenge," in Weber, ed., *Waiting for "Superman,"* 198.

6. Thernstrom and Thernstrom, *No Excuses*, 272–73.

7. Thernstrom and Thernstrom, *No Excuses*, 273.

8. Peter W. Cookson Jr. and Kristina Berger, *Expect Miracles: Charter Schools and the Politics of Hope and Despair* (Boulder, CO: Westview, 2002), 14.

9. It should be noted, however, that high mobility of students in urban districts may render this consistency necessary.

10. Bill Strickland, "How Schools Kill Neighborhoods—and Can Help Save Them," in Weber, ed., *Waiting for "Superman,"* 76.

11. Steven Zemelman, Harvey Daniels, and Arthur Hyde, *Best Practice: Today's Standards for Teaching and Learning in America's Schools*, 3rd ed. (Portsmouth, NH: Heinemann, 2005), viii.

12. Evangeline Lindsley with Nancy Diggs, *My Century: An Outspoken Memoir* (Dayton, OH: Landfall Press, 1997), 176. Ironically Miss Lindsley was a leader in the Ohio teachers' union in the 1940s, fighting such inequities as uneqal pay for women teachers.

13. Thernstrom and Thernstrom, *No Excuses*, 255.

14. Thernstrom and Thernstrom, *No Excuses*, 256.

15. Thernstrom and Thernstrom, *No Excuses*, 258.

16. Mark Gokavi, "Students Getting Free Lunches at School Kept Anonymous," *Dayton Daily News*, March 4, 2010.

17. Chester Finn, Terry Ryan, and Michael B. Lafferty, *Ohio's Education Reform Challenges: Lessons from the Frontlines* (New York: Palgrave/Macmillan, 2010), 37.

18. Harvard Graduate School of Education/Jobs for the Future, "Summary of Preliminary Findings," *Early College High School Study*, June 18, 2004, 2–3.

19. Kalman R. Hettleman, *It's the Classroom, Stupid: A Plan to Save America's Schoolchildren* (Lanham, MD: Rowman & Littlefield Education, 2010), 144.

20. Thernstrom and Thernstrom, *No Excuses*, 56.

21. Thernstrom and Thernstrom, *No Excuses*, 62.

22. Ron Christie, *Acting White: The Curious History of a Racial Slur* (New York: Thomas Dunn/St. Martin's Press, 2010), 225.

23. Christie, *Acting White*, 224.

24. Quoted in Rod Paige and Elaine Witty, *The Black-White Achievement Gap: Why Closing It Is the Greatest Civil Rights Issue of Our Time* (New York: American Management Association, 2010), 71–72.

25. Only recently has it become possible to hire Teach for America corps members in Ohio; it was prohibited up until 2011.

26. Wendy Kopp and Steven Farr, *A Chance to Make History: What Works and What Doesn't in Providing an Excellent Education for All* (New York: Public Affairs, 2011), 72.

27. Julie Landsman, *A White Teacher Talks about Race* (Lanham, MD: Scarecrow Press, 2001), 45.

28. Landsman, *A White Teacher Talks about Race*, 104.

29. Lisa Delpit, *Other People's Children: Cultural Conflict in the Classroom* (New York: The New Press, 2006), 167–68.

30. Delpit, *Other People's Children*, 168.

31. David K. Shipler, *A Country of Strangers: Blacks and Whites in America* (New York: Knopf, 1997) 369–70.

32. James Deneen and Carm Catanese, *Urban Schools: Crisis and Revolution* (Lanham, MD: Rowman & Littlefield Education, 2011), 52.

33. Zemelman, Daniels, and Hyde, *Best Practice*, 297.

34. Jonathan Kozol, *The Shame of the Nation: The Restoration of Apartheid Schooling in America* (New York: Three Rivers Press, 2005), 64–65.

35. Edward T. Hall, *Beyond Culture* (New York: Anchor, 1989), 74.

36. Quoted in Gloria Ladson-Billings, *The Dream-Keepers: Successful Teachers of African American Children*, 2nd ed. (San Francisco: Jossey-Bass Wiley, 2009), 75.

37. Hall, *Beyond Culture*, 203–4.

38. Landsman, *A White Teacher Talks about Race*, 57.

39. Finn, Ryan, and Lafferty, *Ohio's Education Reform Challenges*, 158.

40. Quoted in Ladson-Billings, *The Dream-Keepers*, 96.

41. Hall, *Beyond Culture*, 5.

Part II: Overcoming the Challenges

In this section, we look closely at the people, methods, and visions that have changed the course of the future for DECA students. In a study of five of the world's best school systems, in Finland, Hong Kong, Long Beach (California), Ontario (Canada), and Singapore, the Battelle Institute determined several factors that such schools had in common. They include experiential and collaborative learning, mutual trust between students and teachers, high expectations, a focus on learning rather than accountability, attention to the whole individual, ongoing feedback, and ties to the community. Teachers also have a great deal of latitude in how they reach their goals. In this section we'll see how DECA applies these practices.

What is more, much of what DECA does can be shared with the community. As Principal Dave Taylor says, "It's not about keeping secrets. It's really how do we improve our learning pursuits."

Chapter Six

DECA: The Family

Given the destruction, the violence, and the chaos that students encounter in their neighborhoods, public schools, and sometimes even their homes, what do those at DECA appreciate most?

"It's a safe and loving environment," says Jolena. "For the students as a whole, life at home is so different than it is at school, and when we come to DECA we have a safe environment. I can see it helping everyone; I can see it being beneficial for everyone, like those in trouble, because here we have good friends, and we have a lot of work so it keeps us busy. We get our mind off our home life, and even if it's just for a moment in time, it does help to relieve some of the stress that we have to deal with outside of school."

According to some experts, a safe, supportive, and orderly school environment, along with social and emotional support, is just as important for learning as improving instruction is.[1] In his study of seven outstanding high schools in Ohio, Peter Meyer notes that "safety is perhaps *the* most important ingredient of these successful schools."[2]

What would Dannisha do to change life in the inner city? The first thing she mentions, recalling that her cousin was able to bring a gun to school, is "providing the school environment that is safe." Alonzo, too, is grateful that "in this environment you have people who love you and care about you."

When I tell Shawna that someone—I couldn't recall who—had said that she comes from a dysfunctional family and that DECA is her family, Shawna replies, with a laugh:

That's nearly all of us! That's me. That fits me. This is my second home. When I was at my mother's house, I would get up at almost 4:50 to catch the bus to come here, and I would be one of the last students to leave. And I really did feel like this was my family away from my family, because I feel like they gave me so much that my other family couldn't give me, as far as stability.

I think that's a big thing in an urban school where students who come from shaky homes, if they have stability at school, they have something to look forward to. And I looked forward to that, that coming in and seeing Dr. Hennessey first, because she would be earlier, too, and then seeing my friends and then going from class to class, like there was not much interruption in that stability. . . . And then at home—you just never knew what was going to happen at home, but you knew what was going to happen at school.

Kaneesha, once shuffled from one foster home to another, thinks that "here we decide to put our family issues and poverty issues outside of school, and when we come into school, we decide to be more focused on our work so we can overcome those circumstances and overcome the statistics that people say about disadvantaged students."

For Jewanna, too, school is a refuge from the chaotic atmosphere at home with her numerous siblings and half-siblings. "I love being at school," she says. "This is my favorite home. It hurts me if I don't go to school. I'd rather be at school than at home. I'd rather be around people at school. Home life, I don't know. . . . It's ridiculous at my house."

Although parents may not have been able to offer the ideal home environment, most would like very much for their children to succeed. Andy Smarick cites a survey in which 92 percent of African American parents of all economic levels believed "that a K–12 education that prepares their children was very important," rates that "were higher than for white parents."[3]

Urban parents, says Meyer, "no matter their struggles, want the best for their children. And that is a trait often overlooked in the debate about poverty and education: Low-income parents want the same for their children that high-income parents do—a good education."[4]

Steven Zemelman, Harvey Daniels, and Arthur Hyde advise teachers in the inner city not to assume that parents won't help. "One research project," they say, "showed how some urban teachers grossly underestimated parents' willingness to help their kids or support the teacher's policies. The teachers failed to contact parents whose children were struggling, and when contact was finally made very late in the year, the teachers were surprised at the cooperation and improvement that took place."[5]

Wendy Kopp, founder of Teach for America (TFA), reports that TFA corps members have found that "the vast majority of their students' parents do care and are very responsive to teachers and schools that reach out and show them how to support the educational process."[6] She stresses how important communication and relationship building are to their cooperation.[7]

Parents are important members of the DECA family. As Jolena says, "The teachers here really care about you and your parents are closely involved, so it's like the teachers and the parents have a friendly-type relationship, more than like a business-type relationship, so it's more family oriented."

The engagement of the parents is one factor that differentiates DECA from other schools, Judy Hennessey says. "We demand it, we cajole them and bribe them and praise them, but I see a lot more engagement here than in the upper-income areas where I have worked. I feel the parents definitely are engaged with us. Now, they're more trusting than a [highly educated] population. They're not as well educated as other parents that I've worked with, yet they're asking the right questions. I just think they trust our answers more."

She adds that "parents have to be held accountable, as well as their children. . . . We have all kinds of meetings, [and if] a parent can never be here, then the parent has to agree to choose somebody else: a mentor, a pastor, an aunt—we have all different kinds of people that come in, but still the family is held responsible to have someone here when needed."

At the heart of the DECA family is the "advisory," only roughly similar to a homeroom class. Bryson, a senior, explains: "We have one teacher who we stay with for our entire high school unless we need a change, depending on who works well together, and then we have a small group of students who we are with the whole entire four years. It's like a little family." And it is one that "encourages you and helps keep you on track and also serves as a Good Samaritan when needed."

The advisory consists of a combination of things, he says. "Academic, you know, that comes first. We have these people in the same classes as us, so we can study and talk to each other about problems that we have, as well as we can talk about things going on at home." The advisor is on hand to help, too.

The advisors—and each teacher is also an advisor—are indispensable in maintaining school–parent relations. DECA superintendent Dr. Judy Hennessey explains that "kids know if they're absent that their advisor wants to hear from them, parents know that they have one point of contact to start with. It does clear up a lot of things. It doesn't solve all our problems, but one thing I have noticed is it really minimizes that 'us against them,' so when you do have a discipline situation, almost always we'll contact the advisor and say, 'What do you know is going on in the child's life?' or 'Tell us about your relationship with this family. Who should we approach?' So we don't have this 'Who's trying to get my kid?' mindset that's become so prevalent."

Joe L. Kincheloe and his fellow authors stress how important it is that teachers know what is going on with their students outside the classroom, for "knowing students well, understanding what they are dealing with outside of school, appreciating the problems their parents are facing, and gaining an awareness of what is happening at home that might undermine their ability to concentrate on academic work are the ways critical teachers operationalize a sense of belonging among their students."[8]

Sabrana's mother Lucretia remembers how surprised she was when a teacher at her daughter's new school asked to visit her.

> I had never been to a school where a person came to my house to meet me, and it was the strangest thing when Miss Brown called and said she wanted to come and meet us. We were like, "Why does this lady want to come to our house?"
>
> But then when she came and we met her, it was very helpful for us to transition into DECA. I think that makes a big difference when they go out and meet new families and learn more about their thinking. In a typical classroom, they know nothing about the learning style, the family setup, the structure. All you see is a piece of paper with school work, and that doesn't really tell you anything about the child.

The involvement of teachers, for Lucretia, is one of the best things about DECA: "the fact that if there was something going on in my home, I could e-mail my advisor, who is Miss Brown, and let her know that something's going on with my daughter, and she could tell the rest of the teachers. In a regular school setting, they wouldn't even consider that maybe something's wrong and maybe that's why she's not paying attention in class. I've done that a couple of times," she says, as, for example, when losing her job put added stress on the single mother and her family.

Lucretia knows she can count on the support of Principal Dave Taylor, as well, recalling that when a problem occurred over the summer, "he was able to take care of the situation, on his own time. I've had a really good experience with him."

The idea of family extends to the closeness among students, where competition is replaced by cooperation. The advisory is "like a family," says Kaneesha. "We think about it that way because we're there for each other and there to help each other. Like if one person doesn't know something and needs help, then the other person helps. In my advisory there about four seniors, so we help the younger students in there."

Unlike a homeroom class, the advisory group students range from the ninth to twelfth grades and will be together throughout their school careers. Kaneesha, who grew up in a series of foster homes, thinks she will keep in touch with her advisory group, at least most of them, after she graduates, "because growing up without a family, they feel like family to me."

Small classroom sizes contribute to the feeling of closeness. "Each class broken down holds about fifteen to twenty students," Kaneesha explains, "to help our learning environment, instead of having about fifty kids in a class. Therefore we can have one-on-one sessions during class for help."

Dannisha also appreciates the small class sizes, since they "allow for a more personalized learning, because what you find is that there are ten or fifteen students in a classroom, so you may have five or six students who are really up to par with everything that is going on in class, whereas you may have the other group who need a little more attention, a little more help, so what you can do is assign other students more work so they can get ahead, and also help the other students who need to be caught up. So I feel the atmosphere is one where we don't hold anyone back, but we don't move too fast for the others that need the help."

"Oh, yeah," says Damarion. "Partnership is really big here. A lot of the time students will make little study groups to study for a test that they may have or just come ask another student or a teacher for help on a project or something. So students here, they don't hesitate to ask for help, that's what I should say."

The DECA family is not limited to the advisory group members, nor to one's classmates. Many of the young men have become role models for younger students, like Bryson, who has begun a program to teach the younger boys to become leaders, or like Alonzo, the graduate who frequently returns to encourage those still at DECA. Bryson tells me that Shawna, who had a family background no child should have to endure, was instrumental in forming a group for seventh and eighth grade girls, "to help *them* out!"

Today LaTonya is proud to be president of this girls' mentoring program, called "Phenomenal." She says:

> It's a beautiful thing. One of the things we're focusing on now is sex, which I feel is a very good thing to do, because I feel that there are a lot of things that contribute to a young woman being positive and also that contribute to a young woman being negative. And so if you have this young woman who's in a dysfunctional setting and she's not being taught how to be positive and how to basically learn from her lessons, then she will never know how.
>
> I feel that if some way, somehow, I mentor these young ladies and teach them how to do things in the right way, like having confidence in yourself, being respectful to your body, and truly having that determination to make it out of the expectations, then you'll be more, far more, than the expectations that you leave behind you. That was a passion I developed last year. I've always wanted to do more, but I didn't find that until last year, and so I realized that I want to do this.

At first it was hard to attract participants, but LaTonya persevered. The group now numbers twenty-seven. She sighs as she says:

> It took a lot. First I gave them a schedule of the program and told them how it was going to be run, and things that we were going to talk about, and how it was strictly confidential. To give more credibility I called in professional people who deal with mentoring and specifically [those] who basically want the young ladies to be more positive, so "Now you don't have to listen to the seniors, you can listen to someone who does this twenty-four hours of the day." And I also bring food, which is a plus!

The "family" aspect of DECA has not gone unnoticed by researchers. In a study of DECA and another early-college academies funded by Jobs for the Future, Michael Nakkula and Marie Onaga state that "peer academic support is an additional component of the deep support structure evident at both schools. Such support comes in the form of expectation as well as technical support. The students in both schools push each other to perform at a high level, and many of them spoke in a collective voice when discussing their achievements at the end of high school. They spoke with pride of their peers' accomplishments as well as their own. They spoke of their schools as supportive family institutions—families sharing the common goal of academic and future career success for all the members."[9]

"DECA is more than a school," says Jewel. "They're your family, they're a culture, it's almost a way of life, really. Once you come to DECA, if you graduate from here and go out into life, you can never take out what they've put into you. It's like they say, knowledge can never be taken away from you."

Her friend Vanetta agrees. One of the best things for her was "the whole family aspect." And the family ties continue.

> One of our friends who graduated last year actually wrote us a very nice letter, because, when she came to our university, she wasn't struggling academically, but just trying to find her place socially and just the whole college environment. She wrote Jewel and me a note yesterday, and it was very beautiful, because she said, "I don't think I would be where I am if you hadn't been there." She was like, "The days that it got hard, you held my hand to get through it."
>
> I know for sure that's part of DECA. . . . That support system honestly is what helps you get through, because this experience is not easy, and it's not for everybody, but if you put in the time and if you're willing to open yourself up, it will open a world of doors for you.

The staff, too, is included in the family. As Harvard researcher Karen C. Foster remarked, at DECA "there is little doubt that some students experience teachers and advisors as more committed and caring than family."[10]

For Andre, Dr. Hennessey, the superintendent, "is like a second mom"; he considers his advisor "another mom, also. . . . She knows everything that goes on in my family, and she's like the kind of person that pushes me in classes, and when she sees like I start catching 'senioritis,' or start procrastinating, she's like, 'Know you have deadlines coming up, know what you've got to do, you've got to get to it now, or I'll have to put you in Friday night school.'"

It's not uncommon for the students to call their advisors "Mom," "Dad," "Aunt," or "Uncle"; to Sabrana, her advisor Katy Jo Brown is "Auntie K. J." According to Bryson, "They're just always there, no matter what the problem issue is. We have a lot of teachers here who have taken students into their homes, because they know they are having trouble at home." As in Shawna's case:

SHAWNA'S STORY—CONTINUED

The way I ended up staying with Mrs. A. was: I asked if she would be my advisor, and she said, "Sure." In the beginning I kind of stayed to myself. I didn't speak much, just did my work and went home. There was a lot of drama at home, and she started to see it on my face a lot, so then we began to talk, and I think because of the culture, my mom, and in a lot of families like them, it's always what goes on at home stays at home. You don't speak to anybody at school about what's going on there.

I was very tight-lipped about a lot of things that were going on at home, but eventually I just told her. I was very vague, but I said, "There are a lot of things going on at home, and I can't focus as much as I want to."

When I was at home, the reason I didn't get much sleep is because I would have to come home—and I can't cook in a dirty kitchen, I just refuse to do it— so I would have to clean the kitchen, then I would have to cook the food, then feed the kids in the family, and then clean up those dishes, and then help them a little bit with whatever they need help with, make sure they're bathed, and then do my homework . . .

And, you know, DECA gives an unbelievable amount of work, and some-times I wouldn't even get all that finished—I would come in early and finish the rest—and then take a shower, and then go to sleep, so by that time it was like 12:00, maybe 1:00, and I would get up at 4:50.

Mrs. A. started to take me home with her a few nights a week, and I would stay and do homework and everything until dinner was ready, and it was such a culture shock, because they set the table. That was the first thing, and I was like, "Why are you setting the table? Are you doing this because I'm over here?" And she was like, "No, we sit down at dinnertime and have dinner like a family." So that was my first introduction to a different culture.

And then they left money out. At my house, if you want your money, you won't leave it out. So when I saw that—I knew she knew that I was not a thief or anything—so she felt comfortable leaving money out in front of me. And I said, "Why do you leave money out? That's not smart." So that was another shocker.

Eventually it got to the point where I was missing school and she had to buy me a cell phone, because she had no other way of getting in contact with me to know why I was missing school that day. So she called me, and I let it ring, because I didn't want to tell her that I was missing school because I had to babysit my nephews, because nobody had decided to come home that night.

Eventually she called again, and that last time I picked up and I told her, and she's like, "You know, Shawna, I understand that you feel the need to be there for your family, but that's not your responsibility. You're a child your-self." I felt that I had to make sure that things got done, that the kids ate, bathed, did homework. So my sister finally decided to come home to get her kids, and thirty minutes later Mrs. A. pulled up to take me to school. It was like the last hour of school.

On the way back leaving from school she told me, "I know you're going to be mad at me, but I had to call Children's Services, because that's neglect." I used to just hate that, because it was like "You want me to tell you something?" And my mom would just stay furious with me, so in turn I would get upset with Mrs. A., because now the whole family's mad at me that I said something. So then she said, "And you're coming to live with me." She didn't really ask me, she just said, "You're coming to live with me."

Alonzo, now in college, believes that it is an understatement to say that the staff is like family. He actually had a room at the home of his advisor, and he called the couple "Mom" and "Pop." Sometimes he calls Dr. Hennessey "Grandma." Having grown up without a father, he found other male figures to take that place when he came to DECA. He met Mr. Jones, who, he says, "became like my dad, who I call Dad now. And I met people like [my teacher] Devon Berry and Dave Taylor, who I call my uncles."

Now he's grateful to his former teacher Debney Grey, his "Uncle Debney," for keeping him "on the straight and narrow path." He remembers arguing that

> "I'm doing good. I'm doing better than everybody. Why are you so hard on me?" After class we had like a discussion, and he said, "You're an eagle. Eagles don't fly with buzzards." And he explained how eagles soar and then how buzzards are real low to the ground. And he said, "From now on I want you to stop comparing yourself to other people. Start comparing yourself to yourself."
>
> And when I did that, it was like everything just took off. I was no longer comparing myself with the way he or she did, but I was trying to be the best that *I* could be, and I'm hard on myself, so being the best, even if I fail, I know that I'm still achieving something very great, because I set the bar so high. And that quote—I really appreciate it and I keep it near and dear to me.

Do students sometimes fear that they won't be able to make it or worry about what lies ahead? Alonzo says,

> I always hear that "fear is false evidence appearing real." When you have the love to let you know that the fear is temporary, that you'll get over it, you won't let that fear consume you. Here at DECA, having those individuals, they never let fear be a part [of my life], because they showed me love, giving me advice and being there when I needed them, providing for me when I didn't have . . .
>
> I said it last year, I said I was so happy and grateful that I had an advisor like Ms. Jones. She was literally my everything in the sense that if I was too high, if the ego got too big, she would bring me back down to earth. If I was too low, she would let me know, "You are somebody," and bring me back

even. She was just able to be everything that I needed when I was in high school.

I don't think a lot of youth have a Ms. Jones or a Dr. Hennessey, or a Mr. Berry, or Mr. Jones or Ms. Berry, or Mr. Taylor—everybody doesn't have that, and I was fortunate enough to have that, and you see a difference in your life when you have that at that young age.

Alonzo remembers missing the deadline for enrolling at DECA, but "I came up to Dr. Hennessey and we had a meeting. I owe so much to Dr. Hennessey, because she gave me the opportunity when nobody else did, and I just made the most of it. She let me in the school, and from there I just always felt like at the very least I owe her to do things," he says with a laugh.

She tells the story a lot of times: "Yeah, Alonzo was twelve years old and came up here and talked to me, and I let him in." Sometimes I think if she hadn't let me into DECA, where would I be?

Going back, there are some things that [come up], so even now, people laugh and are like, "You're doing well. What do you wish you could do over?" I'm like, "I just wish that I could do it all over!"

Ties with faculty and staff continue after graduation, too. Jewel, a DECA alum, remembers the closeness with her advisor, Ms. King, who has helped her in so many ways:

Even now, as a college student, I still talk to her, we still kind of mess with each other and talk frequently. She was just asking me how things were going. I told her about school and everything, and then it was like, "Well, how are things *really* going?" like on a personal level, and I was just really honest with her.

At that time I wasn't working or anything like that and I told her I was having some trouble buying my books and this scientific calculator that I needed, and she sent me like a CARE package with some things in it that I needed. She sent me some money to help me in buying these books, she sent me a calculator, just different things like that.

That just really shows that these teachers—you know, you're not just another student to them. They really care about your success and are willing to make sacrifices and do different things for you to see you being successful.

"Because they believe in you," her friend Vanetta explains. "They won't allow your circumstances to determine your outcome in life. They want to give you the resources to learn how to maneuver them."

~~Principal Dave Taylor continues to be an important part of alumni's lives.~~ He reports that

kids just kind of inherently come back and communicate with us. I usually text or call or e-mail the kids. It's pretty easy to stay up with them. If they have a problem, they contact [someone]. There are some who contact me. It really depends on who the kids think they can count on, and when they do that, we do what we can to respond.

Sometimes it's academic stuff, and we tell the kids to come in and we tutor them. We've all done some of that. Sometimes it's just advice. Sometimes it's just "I need to get away," or "I need a meal," or whatever. And the kids will come over, or sometimes they'll just hang out with me and my family for the night, or they'll go shopping with their advisor.

There are a bunch of guys I try to take out for lunch whenever they're in town. They go to school out of town. Once a year or so we'll go out to eat and have a conversation about what's going on in their lives. It's funny—when you leave DECA, you don't really leave DECA. A lot of teachers believe in their DECA kids staying in contact. . . . Our graduates do have a sense of ownership, I think, that they're working not just for themselves in college, mostly for their families, but also for us. They don't want to let us down. They appreciate it and they want to pay forward what we did for them.

NOTES

1. R. M. Katsuyama, "Character Education in Ohio Schools: Results of the Partners in Character Evaluation Study, 1998–2002." Ohio Partners in Character Education, October 21, 2010, www.charactereducationohio.org/utilities/evaluationsummary5-06.pdf.

2. Peter Meyer, *Needles in a Haystack: Lessons from Ohio's High-Performing Urban High Schools* (Washington, DC: Fordham Institute, 2012), 28.

3. Andy Smarick, *The Urban School System of the Future* (Lanham, MD: Rowman & Littlefield Education, 2012), 5.

4. Peter Meyer, *Needles in a Haystack*, 44.

5. Steven Zemelman, Harvey Daniels, and Arthur Hyde, *Best Practice: Today's Standards for Teaching and Learning in America's Schools* (Portsmouth, NH: Heinemann, 2005), 297.

6. Wendy Kopp and Steven Farr, *A Chance to Make History: What Works and What Doesn't in Providing an Excellent Education for All* (New York: Public Affairs/Perseus, 2011), 134.

7. Kopp and Farr, *A Chance to Make History*, 135.

8. Joe L. Kincheloe, kecia hayes, Karel Rose, and Philip M. Anderson, eds., Introduction, *Urban Education* (Lanham, MD: Rowman & Littlefield, 2007), xli.

9. Michael Nakkula and Marie Onaga, "Transitioning to College: Year Four of the E.C.H.S. Study" (Boston: Jobs for the Future and Harvard Graduate School of Education, May 7, 2008), 46.

10. Karen C. Foster and Michael Nakkula, "Early College High Schools: Reconsidering Educational Identity," Harvard Graduate School of Education/Jobs for the Future, December 7, 2004.

Chapter Seven

The Miracle Workers

Unfortunately, not many of us can choose our parents, for when it comes to education, says Dr. Thomas Lasley II, "there's no substitute for the parents and the social capital of the family. The family that you come with—good or bad—it's either gold in your pocket or a cross to bear, and either way, you are either advantaged or disadvantaged in pretty significant ways."

To William A. Sampson, who studied twelve inner-city students with varying academic records, "The family is clearly critical."[1]

The authors of the Coleman Report stated in 1965 that no matter whether students were attending a "good school" or a "bad school," test results correlated with family background. In other words, according to Abigail and Stephan Thernstrom, "It was a student's family—parental education, occupation, income, and race—that made the real difference."[2] Or, as the sociologist Ellen Condit Langemann said, "It's all family."[3]

Is that true? Or can school reform change the situation? Indeed it can, say many, like the researchers Eric Hanushek and Steven Rivkin, who report that schools "can overcome the powerful influence of family and social environment."[4]

Yes, says Eric Hanushek, the Coleman Report had it right: "Families and peers do have a very important influence on learning. But this does not detract from the importance of schools and teachers. On the contrary, it raises their value."[5] As Chester Finn and his coauthors maintain, "The work of schools is surely easier when the rest of children's lives are in good repair, yet when other institutions are pitching in and other policy domains are aligned, schools alone can work wonders."[6]

Educators agree that when it comes to education, teachers—after family influences—are the most important part of the equation, and they can indeed perform miracles. "High-quality teachers can make up for the typical deficits

79

seen in the preparation of kids from disadvantaged backgrounds," Eric Hanushek and Steven Rivkin claim.[7]

According to Steven Brill, Jon Schnur, a driving force behind the Race to
the Top, concluded that failure or success in school had less to do with the
family and community and "more with the teacher in front of the class. Truly
effective teaching, he came to believe, could overcome student indifference,
parental disengagement, and poverty—and, in fact, was the key to enabling
children to rise above those circumstances."[8]

And Wendy Kopp, from her own observations of what Teach for America
(TFA) corps members have accomplished, asserts that "we can solve the
problem of educational inequity through efforts centered within schools."[9]

Do good schools have certain things in common? Yes, says educator
Thomas Lasley II, and "there's no doubt that the teacher is the most important dynamic, so—pretty consistently across the schools that I've seen that
are performing well—you see very, very committed and high-quality teachers. That would be the first thing."

Dave Taylor, principal at DECA, echoes Tom Lasley when he says,
"Number one is the teachers. It just is, any way you want to cut it, any way
you want to slice it. If you have the wrong people on the bus, the bus isn't
going to move. Our teachers are top notch, they work harder, they're smarter,
I'd put them up against anybody in the country. I really would. They're a
higher maintenance bunch than most. They are. I tell them that, but they're
worth it, without question. I think success begets success in a lot of ways.
Having the community behind us really helps enhance a lot what we're able
to do."

Nobody ever said it would be easy, though. As research became available
on the new charter schools in the 1990s, says Brill, it became evident that
"successful teaching was grueling work. It required more talent, more preparation, more daily reevaluation and retooling, more hours in the class day, and
just plain more perseverance than many teachers, and most teachers' union
contracts, were willing or able to provide."[10]

Teachers hold a "tricky place" in the lives of inner-city students, Julie
Landsman thinks:

> We are their advocates, yet also their disciplinarians. We laugh with them, and
> yet, we have to set limits with them. We must make them feel welcome, offer
> them books and pictures, music and ideas that will stimulate them, yet also
> make them feel our disappointment when they don't show up, come late, or
> slough off on a test. We walk a strange line, and often we are not part of their
> community, are not of the same culture.[11]

Although, says Dave Taylor, "people on the outside think that teaching is
a cushy job—you work few hours, you're off summers, you get long
breaks—those kinds of things," it is actually "a very intense job, it's emo-

tionally draining and it requires a good bit of skill." He describes a typical day for a teacher in an urban school:

> When you step into a classroom, they say that the average teacher makes twenty decisions a minute, something along those lines, because when you're in the classroom, you think about it. You're dealing with twenty or twenty-five different personalities. You've got your lesson. You've got to figure out how you're going to squeeze all of your stuff into the class, you've got this kid that has to use the restroom, you've got this kid that's smacking that kid, you've got another kid that's been on something, you've got your principal walking in the door, you've got announcements going over the loudspeaker, always something going on that is trying to keep you from your goal, which is really to get the students to understand the material in front of them.
>
> Of course you can think very hard about what is it that I'm actually delivering and how am I delivering it to the students. How am I getting it to them? So there is a lot that you just have to do, and not just any fool can do it. You can't just put anyone in the classroom and say, "Teach." There's some skill behind it. And some of it's intuitive.
>
> There are some people who intuitively walk into the classroom and say, "This is easy. I know how to do this." Well, that's fine, you're a natural. And that's not always, number one, the best thing, because people who are in that situation don't always continue to grow, because they think they're great, but most people need some guidance on how to structure themselves. And there are certain people who aren't fit to teach, who aren't qualified to be teachers. And those people—you help them and you work with them, but if you can't do the job, you can't do the job. There are no two ways about it.

In a Harvard-sponsored study conducted at DECA, Karen C. Foster and her fellow researcher Michael Nakkula report that the development of skills that have been neglected "requires physical, cognitive, and emotional stamina."

Students described student–teacher relationships as "dramatically different from their previous experiences of adults in school settings. . . . Adults share responsibility for academic success with their students, rather than making demands and then casting negative judgments based on student failure or poor performance. Students are often well aware of performing below grade level and need evidence that teachers will join them, rather than judge them. Providing 'help' is the way in which students describe knowing that their teachers care about them."[12]

Dave Taylor thinks that our local University of Dayton, with its urban teacher academy, does "a decent job. The teachers who usually come out of there, they understand urban students, and that's really the major difference, that they understand the difference between urban learners and suburban learners."

Along with the cultural differences in direct vs. indirect communication that Delpit warns us about, Thomas Lasley II and coauthors Thomas J. Matczynski and James B. Rowley caution that "African American students often respond to a teacher's question using voice, emotion, and nonverbal characteristics. African American students often respond orally, in unison, and in a choral manner based upon traditional modes of verbal expression—oral communication and group participation. If teachers are unaware of their cultural characteristics and historical antecedents, they may interpret this student responsiveness as unruly, disruptive, and unacceptable to the traditional decorum of the classroom." [13]

They add that a black student may lower his head or lower his eyes as reaction to public criticism, which a teacher may interpret as "disrespectful, impolite, and/or rebellious." [14] That same black student might look away when listening, but look directly at an individual when speaking, which, they say, "may help explain the frustrations of European American teachers who often view African American children as belligerent or inattentive based upon student-to-teacher eye contact." [15]

While there are cultural differences between suburban, mostly white students and those, mostly black, in the inner city, they may not be all negative, Tom Lasley says:

> Some people would say black students, African American students, are louder, more vocal. There's a little bit of research to justify that. And, just as an aside, Elizabeth, my daughter who teaches at DECA, would tell you the downside of that is that they're louder and more vocal, the upside is you know exactly where they stand, so there's not the same kind of game-playing. Suburban kids, the upside is they're quieter and more reserved. The downside is they can hate your guts, and they'll tell everybody else but they won't tell you.
>
> So I think, for somebody who's been raised in a suburban white middle-class culture, you've learned certain skills about what to say or not to say to someone else, and if you go into an urban culture and you find this kind of pointed communication, sometimes it's maybe even borderline inappropriate, it's threatening.

DECA counselor Martha Brzozowski looks for the reasoning behind this more outspoken, and disruptive, style of communication. "A lot of the kids here have the mentality that 'if I think something of you, I'm going to say it to you. Otherwise I'm being fake.' They don't really understand the meaning of tact, because they think that if they're being tactful, then they're being fake. They don't really get it."

Although the University of Dayton does a good job, says Dave Taylor,

> Where I take an exception with some of the schools, some of the colleges, is they don't do a good enough job working on classroom management, on understanding a realistic way to manage a classroom. As a young person coming into a different culture, you're not stepping into a [suburban] Center-

ville or Springboro school district. You're coming into a school district or into a school building where in many cases the students run over teachers.

[So you have to] establish expectations. You deal with issues as they come. You learn how to defuse problems when you can. Those discipline issues in a classroom are small and subtle. It's when you don't deal with those small and subtle issues that you get bigger issues.

A kid standing up in the classroom—well, that becomes a kid walking around in the classroom, and that becomes a kid smacking a kid in the head, so when a kid stands up, you tap him on the shoulder and say, "Hey, grab a seat." Or you make a joke about it, but you find a way to defuse things before they become more intense.

And you build relationships with students, but oftentimes college students who are graduating and looking for full-time jobs [as teachers], they view it almost arrogantly, in that they can control the classroom with their personality. That just saying to a kid, "Hey, stop!" is going to do it. They don't always understand that they have to be more organized in the way that they control their classrooms.

The biggest thing for a teacher is how do you spend your first day in your first week. If you don't spend time at the beginning of the year establishing your expectations for how your class is going to run, if you don't spend time working on the procedures of what students are expected to do: How do you ask to go to the restroom? How do you get permission to sharpen a pencil? Or how do you turn papers in?

If you don't cover those things with your students on the very first day of school, you're in for a long year, because what's going to happen is, you'll have that kid who's always really annoying who knows you didn't cover that stuff, he's going to stand up and say, "Hey! You didn't tell me I couldn't stand up and sharpen my pencil whenever I want to!" "Well, you should have known that." "Well, you didn't tell me to."

So you spend your first day going over that stuff so that it's all kind of laid out. I don't know if schools of education spend enough time going over those things, but that's what leads to teacher burnout. [So many teachers] get in and then they realize how much work it is and how difficult it is.

DECA teachers tend to have more independence than those at many schools, Dave explains, which is one of the reasons why it is important to hire good teachers. He describes the process. If the resume appears suitable, the next step would be interviews with him and with DECA faculty members, who will join with Dave and discuss how they would rank the candidate. The second step would be a demo lesson in front of a group of students for their opinions, followed by another interview to address any concerns the applicant may have. After checking references, a hiring decision is made.

Tom Lasley, the retired dean of education at the University of Dayton and DECA founder and board member, describes the hiring advantages that DECA has compared with larger schools. Number one, he says, the school is able to more thoroughly reference-check the applicant, so they have a deeper understanding of who the person is. Number two, they make them teach a lesson—they actually come in and teach a lesson. As a result, they can see how you teach content and interact with kids. That happens very infrequently in education, where you would come in and you would actually teach.

You can understand that in a Dayton public school or in [suburban] Centerville, where some years they may be hiring lots of teachers, it's perceived as practically impossible. So DECA has been able, I think, to do a better job of ensuring the quality of teachers that it has because it knows more about the people before it hires them and then it watches them actually interact with kids and teach content before they make a final decision to hire them. So they know a lot more about them.

In spite of the many demands made on DECA teachers, Dave Taylor says:

We never have a shortage of applicants. I don't know that we've ever had a situation where we haven't had a bunch of applicants. It's not always easy to find the right fit. That leads into another question that you ask, "What kind of person do you look for?" We're an inner-city school, so you've got to look for classroom management. You've got to look for somebody who knows how to maintain an organized room and knows how to control students within that.

We go for people who are competent in their content, so much so in fact that they're not going to need someone holding their hand, giving them, you know, "OK, here's the pacing guide. Here's what you cover on day one." We have had people like that who have come here, and they haven't done well, because you have to figure out what to do on your own. You can't have someone telling you what to do every second of every day.

Now, beyond that we look for people who will build strong relationships with students. A teacher who knows how to get students to listen and knows how to empathize with students is more effective than someone who sets themselves up as a dictator or a tyrant in the classroom and doesn't do a good job making the kids see that they're a real person. That's why we ask the kids. We want to see what their perspective is on the teacher.

And I guess we also want to see someone who's incredibly passionate about what they do. People who work here need to work harder. If you come into this job assuming that you're going to come in at 8:15 and leave at 4:00, you're probably not going to do a good job. And so people have to understand that your role as a teacher is something where these kids are counting on you to help make a difference in their lives. If you're in it for the summers and you're in it for the short hours, you're working at the wrong school.

From DECA's earliest days, Tom Lasley confirms, the notion of close connections between teachers and students was stressed. Today it is one of the salient characteristics of the school and a leading cause of its success.

We'll recall that every teacher not only instructs but also acts as advisor to a group of a dozen or so students; the "advisory" formed of this group will remain the same, with the same leader, throughout the student's career. Judy

Hennessey, former principal and current superintendent, stresses how important the advisory system is:

> It's woven into the way we structure our day and the way we hire our staff and in the expectations that we share with parents that this will be a place where their child is known and accountable and that there will be at least one advocate. We call those the advisors.
>
> It is truly part of our structure that not only are they licensed and qualified to teach their content, but they also have to be a surrogate parent to about twelve to sixteen kids. They get to know them and they're their champions, they're disciplinarians, they're the primary contact with the family, and that is probably pivotal to any success that we're having. . . .
>
> The students know they can bring their burdens from home and somebody's in their corner listening. Just the listening is important, so the personalization is a key, and it's all through the literature on kids in poverty. I do believe that the Gates Foundation, which insisted on some type of personalized high-school structure—they were right.

It's hard to believe that this very attractive blue-eyed, dark-haired dynamo is old enough to be the grandmother of five. "Sweet, very sweet," is how Damarion describes her, but, he adds, "She's tough." As she passes through the hallway, she might stop to hug a student, or call to another, "Honey, I hear you did a good job on that English paper." Or she might be confronting a remorseful teen in her office. "Tears don't work on me," she says sternly.

Like other members of the staff, Judy works long hours. "Dr. Hennessey, she's *always* working," says Bryson, "and people see that. She's not only handling school things, but she's trying to make sure that we're able to finish our [school-required 'Gateway' programs], she's doing senior nights to get us in here and give us the time to do it. If I need a ride home, she takes me there, so that I'm able to get work done. She's really the glue that helps keep the school together."

Andre recalls that when he fell behind in the fourth quarter of his junior year, Dr. Hennessey would pick him up at 7:00 in the morning so that he could be at school at 7:30 and begin work early in order to catch up. All the teachers "work very hard and they let us see that they work hard so that we can step up and do what we need to do," he adds.

She takes her responsibilities very seriously. There are nights when she worries about her charges. Is a student showing signs of parental abuse? Are some of the seniors aiming too high in their college expectations, setting themselves up for disappointment? Does one of the very poor families have enough to eat? When a student was caught stealing snacks, it was indeed because there was not enough food at home; Judy saw that the family was directed to the proper social services.

A social worker/family advocate, available three days a week, helps facilitate such decisions, as does Martha Brzozowski, "Miss Martha" to the students, DECA's onsite mental-health therapist/counselor. In addition to dealing with individual problems that arise, Martha conducts an anger-management course and oversees a peer-mediation program run by students well trained in the process.[16]

DECA graduate Vanetta remembers how she struggled with math and science in high school, and that "whatever it was, whether it was preparing for the OGT [Ohio Graduation Tests] or whatever, [the teachers] were there on Saturdays, they were there on Sundays, they were there at the school. Even when I didn't know and I'd get frustrated, they still believed in me."

LaTonya appreciates "the one-to-one connection with the teachers. You know, they're willing to come in early and they're willing to stay late. They give you their cell phone numbers and many times their house phone numbers, just in case you have any questions with school or need advice with home life."

Sabrana, too, has learned to rely on the availability of her teachers when she's having problems. "I think the atmosphere is awesome," the fourteen-year-old says. "I feel comfortable, I feel safe. I do like that. I feel like I can go to school and if I really need somebody to talk to, I can go to Miss Brown and boo-hoo it out. Or I can go to Miss Jordan's room and cry and cry, I feel so comfortable."

Teachers also make themselves available for discipline duties. In what might appear to be as much of a punishment for the teacher as for the student, tardy arrivals must make it up in triplicate, "so if you're late an hour, you have to make up three hours," Damarion explains. "You can either come in early in the morning before school starts or stay after school for a couple of hours to make up time, but you have to be under the supervision of a teacher."

Then there is the dreaded "Friday night school," also under staff supervision, where students are punished by participating in boring activities like standing at attention or marching in circles, all to the tune of loud bagpipe music!

Jolena speaks of how, if you are a struggling student, "you can stay after school, you can come in early. I know that last year when I had to make up my time, I used to come in with my teacher on Sundays, and we used to do work. . . . They are very dedicated. They're here Monday through Sunday. . . . They even have their own individual cell phones. They encourage you to call them at home if you need help with homework. We have advisor parties, where we go to teachers' homes and we just kind of hang out, and just get to know each other on a personal level. Sometimes they take students out to eat or to dinner, things like that."

Dave Taylor stresses the importance of advisors' spending time with students "in a low-pressure, nonacademic way, where they can kind of do some team-building stuff" and allow the students to see their teachers "as more than just the person who is going to boss me around for the next nine months or so."

Although Dave never knows what his day will bring, he, too, can count on a workday that will last at least twelve hours, whether he is attending meetings outside or inside the building, working on a project in his office, supervising a classroom, or "circulating the building, keeping an eye on everyone in the hallway and the cafeteria." All of which Dave, an African American who became principal in his late twenties, does with a quiet air of authority that belies his young age.

"You're always juggling a lot of different things," he says, "but I like to think of myself as the keeper of the flame, the person who is trying to keep us focused on what our basic goals are, what our big targets are and holding [everyone] accountable to make sure we're doing those things."

He sees his job as one of "keeping my eyes on the big picture and then making sure that I and the staff spend our time working on that. . . . I've got goals for the staff, for myself for the year. And I want to communicate that to the entire faculty. I want us to continuously go back to those things and make sure that when we take on new projects, when we start doing this, doing that, it all relates to our big goals for the year." Dave is not alone in his task of creating a vision for DECA. A staff "Transformation Committee" meets regularly to brainstorm on plans for the future.

Dave admits, though, that it's not easy working with urban students,

> students who are saying they want to go to college, because if you look at the suburbs, where there's a stable home and all the resources that are available to a child, many times those kids still don't go to and finish college. So this is not an easy undertaking. This is nothing where it's as simple as saying we'll make this thing happen.
>
> There's a lot of work that has to go into it from the students, the parents, and the school. It really is a team effort, and that's the beauty of the school that we recognize that and rather than hide behind excuses, it's "OK, if we would eliminate every possible obstacle, what would keep you from going to college? Let's give you the resources you're going to need." It's a special place that way.

It may be to DECA's advantage that teachers and staff members tend to be young, at least some students think so. As Jewel says, "It's the best, because you feel they're on your level. Even though they're older than you, even though we call them parents, you kind of feel like they're older siblings and so you can be more honest with them. They feel more like mentors, so you don't have that hierarchy that you have with your parents, where you don't want to share and you don't want to open up. With them you feel comfortable to open yourself up."

Damarion likes it that the young teachers are "real laid back. They're serious, but not too serious to where they're griping at the students to do this or that, because when you come at a student like that, it makes the student not even want to work. I know how teenagers can be at like fifteen or sixteen, when they feel like 'you're not my mom or dad, so you can't tell me what to do.' Like I was saying, they're real laid back, and the way they approach how they teach makes the student want to learn, and helps them learn."

Bryson, too, notes that here "they have a lot of younger teachers. Some of them are fresh out of college with that drive to teach, teach, teach somewhere . . . They're not perfect—I'm not going to say that—but they have the will, and that kind of shows through." One teacher, especially, Mrs. Cameron, has inspired him to want to be a teacher.

Alonzo thinks of the school system in the affluent suburb of Oakwood as a well-oiled machine, but, he says, "DECA's working our way toward being a well-oiled machine, because we have teachers that care and are very intelligent and that are young, which makes them able to relate to the students, because the age difference is not that great."

TFA's Wendy Kopp also sees advantages in having young teachers: "It can make a huge difference to channel the energy of young people, before they know what's 'impossible' and when they still have boundless energy, against a problem that many have long since given up on."[17] It makes sense, though, that those with less experience should be able to count on support from other teachers and from experienced teacher/coaches, the kind of help that DECA provides.

The spirit of teamwork at DECA extends to relations among staff and teachers. Teaching can be a lonely job, as Judy Hennessey describes: "You're in your classroom, you close your doors, you kind of hunker down. We don't have very many doors here. You can hear the teachers around you, and there's a lot more technical discussion among the teachers: 'Who's doing this activity? How did it work? Are you able to get to this kid? I'm frustrated, etc., etc.' so I think the teachers sustain each other, more than I've seen at other schools. It's very helpful because I think [working with] a needy population can suck the life out of you."

In addition to informal communications, there are monthly meetings of different cohorts of teachers—those who teach students of the same age—as well as monthly meetings of those who teach different subjects. Since "they all meet at the same time in different parts of the building," Dave Taylor says, he makes it a point to stop in at various meetings and ask questions.

He credits the frequent meetings with keeping the teachers motivated:

I think they energize each other, I really do. I think the kids take energy, and they give energy. I think for a lot of our teachers, they see tangibly what they do. They see the value they bring. I guess there are several things.

The autonomy that we give them as administration is really liberating of a teacher, to know that "I'm respected enough to do what I'm supposed to do and just produce" is a liberating thing. I'm not going to have someone lording over me, saying, "Did you do this page? Did you do this same page? Get it done and show it me," that's all you've got to do. That, I think, teachers really respond well to.

Working closely with other adults who are intelligent, hardworking and committed is something that's really encouraging to our teachers, as well, that they really enjoy, because they know that it's not just about me and I'm not in this alone. If I've got an issue with this kid, I can go to so-and-so and ask them, "Hey, what are you doing that works?"

We do a good amount of celebrating together. We do celebrate our successes, we party a little bit together, but I think the faculty here knows how special a place this is and knows that the impact that they're making here may not be the same as it would be if they were somewhere else. There they may not be able to do some of the things they do here.

Teachers can also count on the help of two teaching coaches, Kanika Jones and Michelle Szucs, who are well trained in methods of implementing instructional strategies, and whose peer coaching "consists of our coteaching and modeling lessons." They also conduct workshops for professional development, where they might discuss such things as a "common language" to develop cohesiveness among the staff.

They stress that they are there to coach, rather than evaluate, and to assist with specific problems a teacher might have. Kanika describes what a classroom visit might entail. First she or Michelle will have asked the teacher what problems or ideas he or she would like to focus on. "For example, a teacher might feel she can't keep the class on task, or there is too much time (or not enough) in going from one activity to another. Implementation and follow-through might be an issue. Are they getting the students to think on different levels?" Everything is confidential, she says, and there is no paper trail:

Trust is a very important part of the process. It is important that the staff be open and willing. The demeanor of the coaches and their rapport with the staff is important. You can't be judgmental, nor can you be a softie. You cannot be standoffish to be effective, so personality is important. You can explain how to improve without being offensive.

When I go to visit a teacher, if she wants me to look specifically at these three things, what that does is make it less subjective, because when I go there, I won't look at Johnny hanging off the ceiling, or Amanda or whoever doing whatever. I'm focusing specifically on what she wants me to look at and what typically happens when we discuss from the notes what was observed, is that we can pinpoint at what point in the lesson did things kind of turn and when the kids did what they did.

Not so much, "Oh, she was bouncing on her seat, asking questions out of turn," but rather was it that the instructions weren't clear? Was there a lag in transitioning time? Were the activities too hard in the beginning and too easy at the end, so could they have been reversed? It just really allows us to focus on the lesson ahead and allows us to figure out what behavior we can alter as a result of the lesson, rather than "You did this, you did this, and you did this, and that's why they did that." It just takes the subjectivity out of it, so that's where we are right now. . . . We're actually observing them from things that they want us to look at.

The next phase will be going into each other's classrooms now, so we'll be out of it, and the teachers will pick a partner who is not in their cohort or in their content level. You know, typically people feel comfortable speaking with people in their own content level.

It really went well last year. We had veterans pairing with novice teachers, social studies pairing with English, math pairing with language arts. It was really interesting to look at the people and who they were paired with and the questions that they were able to come up with, and again, they utilized it too, because now that we've used it with them, they know how to use it, and that's basically just the scaffolding technique.

So now when we say we are coming to do rounds, they'll know, and the premise is that if everything goes right, when other people come in from the outside, and we say, "We have a group coming to do rounds, who's available?" They'll automatically go, "I need to have my lesson planned, I'm going to have a preconference, here are the questions I want to look over for it," and it won't be too foreign for them having people in the classroom. It's really cool.

The notion of collaboration extends to compensation, as well. In addition to their salaries, teachers receive a board-mandated bonus awarded on the merits of the group.

Although they earn pay comparable to that of other schools, or slightly more, could they make more at other places? "Absolutely," says Dave Taylor. Why, then, do they stay at DECA?

For Michelle Szucs, the best thing about DECA is "opportunities. There are so many opportunities, for both students and teachers. Everyone has an opportunity here to be a leader, accept challenges, step up and take on different leadership roles, be on different committees. In traditional public schools there may not be that many opportunities."

As Katy Jo Brown, a science teacher, says:

Who wouldn't stay? Yes, it's hard, and time consuming, and exhausting, but I'm already dreading the day that I may have to leave. As soon as a teacher steps in the building, they know their voice will be heard. Their thoughts are expected to be shared and everyone values their input. . . . We work hard together and make time to play hard together as well. I was sent on three trips with coworkers my first year to become a better teacher. I always know that when I bring a concern to an administrator, I will be heard. I know that if I have a concern about a student, someone will help me find the resources to assist them better.

Every day I know everyone in the building is working just as hard as I am and we are all here to help the students be successful. I love being able to walk out of my room between classes and reflect with a fellow teacher on how the class period went and how I can improve. Being able to hear what the senior English, first-year history, seventh-grade history, and seventh-grade English classes are learning all at the same time is powerful.

We are learning from each other and sharing values and techniques without even leaving the classroom.

Being expected to visit the homes of our new students to ensure a well-rounded idea of what our students face is powerful. Having an advisory where I get to spend forty minutes a day with a student makes both of us better people. I learn more about my students and what they face in that time together than they could ever learn from me about what their future entails. I can't imagine being anywhere else.

Her colleague Sarah Sims has stayed at DECA because "I had never seen a group of people so dedicated and committed to the success of their school and their students. DECA is a family and so much more than a place of employment or a school. Through DECA we have the power to help students succeed who might have otherwise fallen through the cracks due to poverty or family situation. This is a powerful thing."

Katie King, who teaches math, believes that

the kids make it worth it. . . . I love that I am allowed to be creative and try to solve problems. I feel that DECA allows me to truly try to change the world, and not just one kid at a time . . . I work with the most incredible staff—no one is selfish, no one is clique-ish, and everyone works so hard to make sure these kids succeed. I am trusted to make decisions that affect curriculum and policy.

I have fun here. I have fun with the staff. The fact that we work with all aspects of the students, and not just their grades, reminds me how complex human life is in general, and how that makes educating students a very complicated job. Knowing the students as more than a number makes the thank-you's that I receive from them so powerful.

The staff respects one another because, even though we may not be friends under other circumstances, we know that each of us is here because we want the students to be successful in life, and all of our intentions are in alignment. At the same time, the diversity of ideas on HOW to get the students to be successful challenges me to constantly think outside the box.

Gloria Ladson-Billings describes the good teacher who shows respect and kindness toward students,[18] but many DECA teachers express a stronger emotion: love. "I have come to love the kids and feel a personal responsibility to them all" . . . "I genuinely love my students and coworkers and leaving would be abandoning them" . . . "I tell my students all the time, 'I love you, but sometimes I don't like the things you do.' They understand that my love is unconditional . . ." "It all comes down to loving the kids."

* * *

And the kids? Perhaps they, too, can be called miracle workers, for it is their drive and determination—what Paul Tough calls "grit"—that help them succeed where others fail. "At times it can be overwhelming," says Bryson. The students have "all this DECA burden, on top of burdens at home. A lot of these students struggle with abusive parents, parents with drug addictions, a lot of us have to take care of our homes. We have so much stuff to do that sometimes it becomes a burden."

"But," he adds, "at the same time I understand what DECA has to do. They have to instill in us in four years what a lot of these students in suburban areas learned their whole lives. They have to teach us networking and professionalism and then catch us up, because most of us have skill gaps. A lot of us come in with fourth-grade levels in reading and writing and math. They have to do all this in four years, so it is a lot."

The students agree that DECA students are not smarter, they just try harder, and those with family problems, says Bryson, "are some of the hardest working people you'll ever meet." In LaTonya's opinion, "Many people who come from a dysfunctional family succeed more, for one, because they have the determination to make it out, because they do realize that if they don't make it out, then they will always be in that dysfunctional setting."

"I would say that a lot of us are determined to succeed because we have nothing else," says Dannisha. "Failure is really not an option, because you know that you are either going to succeed or you're going to end up falling behind. And you know there's no question what's going to happen if you fail. You know exactly where you're going to be. You're going to be right with the people who you see every day and so you're faced every day with the reality that if you fail, you're stuck here." Jolena shares the same motivation: "My parents' background—that also motivates me to want to do more, become more, and achieve more in life."

For such busy students, time management is a big issue, Andre says, and "you've got to have the drive for it, or you're not going to make it." But he appreciates being kept busy, "so my time isn't being used for unnecessary things like things that won't get me somewhere in my future, and being at DECA, it really pushes you. It also keeps me always doing something, so my time is used for doing positive things instead of negative."

"I think one thing about the school is that even though every student in here is different, we're all working to achieve the same goal," Damarion says. "We all want to go to college, we all want to make something of ourselves, and we all want to work hard to get there. We come to DECA, it makes us work hard." He, too, believes that DECA students are not smarter than others, but, he says, "I would say maybe they have more motivation than those other students who couldn't stick through it, or maybe [those who left] just didn't have as tough a mindset."

One of the questions that Daron frequently gets as a Student Ambassador is, "So, do you all pick the cream of the crop?" And, he says,

> My response to that is always, "Absolutely not." I say, "It's not about them being smart, it's about having drive . . . and perseverance," because you need diligence, you need hard work, arduous work, but drive is the most important part, of course, in coming here. So when you have drive amongst the teachers, amongst the students, and drive amongst the administration and the rest of the other faculty, you get a school like DECA, where we all know that common goal and everybody works with everyone to get to that common goal, which is to get to college.

DECA students consider themselves "more focused," rather than "smarter."[19] "We have some students who are really smart and some students who are kind of behind," Bryson notes,

> But you can say we're more determined, and we work harder than anyone else. [DECA students] know when they come here that they're going to have to work hard, but students who have the most potential end up coming here, applying.
> But then we have a lot of people who attrition to other schools, because they give up. So in fact you weed out the people who don't want to do it or who aren't able to. But they will tell you that a lot of students try to come back, because they recognize what DECA is doing."

He adds, taking ownership of the school as so many students do, "A lot of students who leave ask to come back, but we can't do that."

Jewel explains that neither she nor her friend Vanetta "is the smartest, like on a test. What DECA teaches you is that 'no' is pretty much not in your vocabulary. Or 'can't.' And DECA teaches you that if you don't know the answer, that's OK, but you must find it out. That's why I say DECA doesn't have the smartest kids. They're not smarter, it's just that they align them with the resources to get where it is that they're trying to be. And so that's really it."

Alonzo sums it all up: "When you have educated, young enthusiastic teachers who are willing to do anything to see their students make it and then you have students who may not have all the exposure, but they have the work ethic and the desire, you have the best of both worlds, and that's what makes DECA, DECA."

NOTES

1. William A. Sampson, *Black Student Achievement* (Lanham, MD: Rowman & Littlefield Education, 2002), 202.

2. Abigail Thernstrom and Stephan Thernstrom, *No Excuses: Closing the Racial Gap* (New York: Simon & Schuster, 2003), 217.

3. Quoted in Thernstrom and Thernstrom, *No Excuses*, 217.

4. Diane Ravitch, *The Death and Life of the Great American School System: How Testing and Choice Are Undermining Education* (New York: Perseus/Basic Books, 2010), 182.

5. Eric Hanushek, "The Difference Is Great Teachers," in Karl Weber, ed., *Waiting for "Superman": How We Can Save America's Failing Public Schools* (New York: Public Affairs, 2010), 82.

6. Chester E. Finn Jr., Terry Ryan, and Michael B. Lafferty, *Ohio's Education Reform Challenges: Lessons from the Frontlines* (New York: Palgrave/Macmillan, 2010), 159.

7. Quoted in Ravitch, *The Death and Life of the Great American School System*, 181.

8. Steven Brill, *Class Warfare: Inside the Fight to Fix America's Schools* (New York: Simon & Schuster, 2011), 2.

9. Wendy Kopp and Steven Farr, *A Chance to Make History: What Works and What Doesn't in Providing an Excellent Education for All* (New York: Public Affairs/Perseus), 2011, 30.

10. Kopp and Farr, *A Chance to Make History*, 1–2.

11. Julie Landsman, *A White Teacher Talks about Race* (Lanham, MD: Scarecrow Press, 2001), 118–19.

12. Karen C. Foster and Michael Nakkula, "Early College High School: Igniting and Sustaining Educational Identity Development," Harvard Graduate School of Education and Jobs for the Future, December 7, 2004, 18.

13. Thomas J. Lasley II, Thomas J. Matczynski, and James B. Rowley, *Instructional Models: Strategies for Teaching in a Diverse Society*, 2nd ed. (Belmont, CA: Wadsworth/Thomson Learning, 2002), 44.

14. Lasley, Matczynski, and Rowley, *Instructional Models*, 381.

15. Lasley, Matczynski, and Rowley, *Instructional Models*, 45.

16. The social worker is called "family advocate" and the mental-health therapist, "counselor," terms that are deemed to sound less threatening to students and parents.

17. Kopp and Farr, *A Chance to Make History*, 178.

18. Gloria Ladson-Billings, *The Dream-Keepers: Successful Teachers of African American Children*, 2nd ed. (San Francisco: Jossey-Bass/Wiley, 2009), 73.

19. Foster and Nakkula, "Early College High School," 24.

Chapter Eight

Academics

Anthropologist Edward T. Hall, remarking on the traditional instructional methods of higher education, notes that "most universities are very expensive ways of educating professors."[1] He calls today's schools "a vignette of how man . . . has managed to ignore or disregard some of the most compelling aspects of his own nature."[2]

Because we, too, are primates, he says, not only do we benefit from working in small groups, but primates do "most of their learning from peers, and man is no exception"; many people learn best by teaching others. He complains that in the current circumstances, "school life is an excellent preparation for understanding adult bureaucracies," but not for learning.[3]

DECA does it differently. With a teacher on hand to facilitate, students do not hesitate to help one another, as Andre describes: "A friend of mine, right now he's doing a PowerPoint so I'm helping out, because I previously did it. So sometimes if a person has done something before, they can help you out on it, and in classes, if you're not understanding it, you can ask a friend and they'll help you. One of my friends helped me in my sophomore year in my math class, because I was having a problem with it, so he helped me a lot there."

Thomas Lasley and his coauthors agree that students do not reach their full potential under the traditional "I talk, you listen, and you learn" kind of instruction, as Adam Urbansky describes it, for it has been shown that "people remember about 10% of what they hear, 20% of what they see, 40% of what they discuss, and 90% of what they do."[4]

Within the framework of what one Harvard study called the school's "relational approach to education," DECA's teachers make learning relevant to their students' lives through the "enjoyment of interactive, hands-on learning."[5] And it's effective: research shows that "students whose teachers conduct hands-on learning activities outperform their peers by about 70% of grade level in math and 40% of grade level in science."[6]

In science class, the students might be learning about kinetic energy, putting together a miniature roller coaster to learn how marbles behave on the curves. In math class they might be learning in context, rather than in the abstract, by building a model house. Combining algebra and geometry, the exercise includes calculating areas and volumes, as well as interest rates in a real contract. Kaneesha describes the project:

> We build our houses with clay, but first we go out into a real community and measure the distance around houses and how tall they are and things. When we get back to school we write down all the calculations and try to create it so that the house would have to be smaller and able to fit on the table. We create the basement first, and then the first floor, depending on the kind of house the teacher assigned to you.
>
> There would be three or four people in a group. We all work together as a team, so we don't literally assign different people assignments, or else one student would be doing all the work, so here we split the work up evenly and, according to how the house is, we build them with however many floors the house is supposed to have, how big the house is, then the students get to paint them, put the roofs on with glue, hot glue—some kids burned themselves—but that's how we create the house.

She adds that most of the classes are creative and include student participation, for example:

> I just heard recently that in science the teacher had one of those static electricity balls that you touch and it shocks you. He was teaching the students about electricity, so he decided to bring that in to let them touch it and see how electricity flows. In Spanish today we did "graffiti"—not really graffiti—but the teacher had posters up everywhere with questions on them, so we could go up there and write the answers in different colors.
>
> In language arts we're working on our autobiographies, book reflections, and also on Optimist Club essays. They're for scholarships. She's making it a demanding requirement for us to do. It's not optional anymore.
>
> In Mrs. Cameron's class the students will read a book and then they'll watch a movie about the book and compare and contrast them. Right now they're studying *The Crucible.* They just finished the book and now they're watching the movie.

Here relevance, too, is a major factor. Jolena tells me that when her class was studying Shakespeare, the same teacher had her students "recreate one of the themes and put a modern spin to it."

Language arts is one of Bryson's favorite subjects: "I love to be creative, write papers. I like a lot of the themes in there, Greek mythology, Shakespeare, and things like that. My teacher actually helped us gain a love for

Shakespeare. We always joke about 'these little black kids like Shakespeare!' It's a little joke that goes around, because we're not ever exposed to it. We talked about the same emotions and things in Shakespeare's time and applying that to real life, or to present-day life."

Students can apply what they have learned by participating in Robotics competitions or in the statewide Mock Trial program, or in the state oratorical contest, in all of which DECA students have excelled.

Again, nobody said teaching would be easy, though. "Good teaching is hard work," say Lasley, Thomas Matczynski, and James Rowley, who stress the importance of planning and setting goals. "It requires thought, reflection and creativity."[7] And Allan Ornstein and Lasley speak of "the learning paradigm" based on how children really learn. "Learning paradigm teachers get outside themselves . . . and get inside the minds of the *students*: How do *they* learn? How do *they* construct knowledge? How do *they* make sense of the world? How can I, as the teacher, participate in the learning process with my students?"[8] In such classes, they say, "students become active learners rather than teacher-controlled intellectual pawns."[9]

Fortunately, there are many strategies available, embodied in, among other things, the NCNSP [North Carolina New Schools Project] Common Instructional Framework, under which "every student reads, writes, thinks and talks every day." These include: Collaborative Group Work, Writing to Learn, Literacy Groups, Questioning, Scaffolding, and Classroom Talk.

Within these guidelines there are tricks to the trade that teachers can use to engage students. For example, teaching coach Kanika Jones describes a "gallery walk," one of the activities that DECA promotes. It may be preceded by an introductory activity in which a teacher might read a segment of a text or show a film. Questions are posted around the room on chart papers for small groups of students to answer. A "carousel" is a similar activity, as two or three students move from one poster to the other. In a science class focusing on measurement, a particularly humbling example for outside observers was a poster with instructions to "give an everyday example of the difference between 'precision' and 'accuracy.'"

Kanika Jones describes another learning method:

> A "fishbowl" activity is more of a discussion activity, in which you can have students generate questions, so if there are twenty students in class, you can create two concentric circles and the inner circle faces each other, and they're the only people who are allowed to talk. The outside circle listens to the inside and they take notes, so when the teacher is asking them questions: "What do you think so-and-so's life was about?" or "How do you think that could affect him in the future?" the kids develop a dialogue, but then the thing is, the students on the outside who think they are missing something or want to make a point, their only job is to write.

Then what they do is switch turns. The outside circle becomes the inside circle, and they can expound upon what the other students said, or reiterate, or they can say, "They forgot this point." It's just to kind of further their critical thinking skills.

When we mention an activity, the kids all say, "Oh, wow! We did that in Mrs. So-and-So's class." For us to hear them saying that, then that means that a lot of the teachers are utilizing these strategies.

Such strategies were not immediately embraced by students and faculty, though:

Initially when [fellow coach] Michelle and I started to do the coaching and we were implementing to actually meet with the teachers, the new students wouldn't want to participate because they had never been taught how to think or allowed to think. I mean, when you think about it, they're coming from schools where everything is either multiple choice, true and false, fill in the blank, short answer.

So now when they come here, they're looking at these, and they're just like "What do you want us to do?" It took a while. There was a transition with the teachers as well as the students, and to see everybody on the same page now and actually going to another level has been phenomenal.

DECA students who come from traditional schools often "can't think very well," Judy Hennessey says.

One of the things we've really tried to stretch the envelope with is asking the types of questions both on our tests and in the classrooms that really cause kids to have to apply what they're learning. It is so hard to do that, because you get caught up in wanting them to get the right answers, wanting to cover the material. It's hard to stop and make sure that the whole point of the lesson is: "Do you know why you're learning this?" And "Can you use this in a similar situation?" Our kids are really weak at that, more so than suburban kids, because they have not been taught.

I think a lot of times when parents don't know better, they let teachers just do a "drill and kill" kind of class. You do the problems—you do a hundred of them—but you wouldn't have a single idea how to apply that, or you memorize things that you can get at your fingertips off the Internet. Memorizing is not necessarily appropriate for that set of information. It's changing, anyway. But we see a lot of kids coming to us, and they actually get combative, verbally upset, when we force them to think.

Kanika Jones explains that

the whole thing behind these strategies is really just to facilitate. That's what the teacher should do anyway, just monitoring the kids, that's all it is, and at the end facilitating discussions based on what the kids can come up with.

Typically in the past—and we've had some teachers say this to us—they teach the way they were taught to, or they teach the way they were taught to teach in college methods classes in college: all the kids sit in a row, work by yourselves, [the teacher talks], you take notes.

For some it was hard for them to let go of that control, because they were so fearful of "I've never worked with kids in groups. What if they get too loud? I've never done this, what if this happens?"

What our teachers found out is, if it's in order and if the instructions and directions are very direct, you won't have the issues, and actually those teachers who were fearful in the beginning are some of our best teachers when it comes to implementing group work.

Similar to the NCNSP's Common Instructional Framework, "Best Practices" is the term that Steven Zemelman, Harvey Daniels, and Arthur Hyde use for methods they claim will achieve high standards of learning. Best Practices, they explain, "is a *philosophy*—a set of harmonious and interlocking *principles of learning*." These principles include "Small-Group Activities, Reading as Thinking, Representing-to-Learn, Classroom Workshop, Authentic Experiences, Reflective Assessment, and Integrative Units."[10] They, too, lead toward "shift[ing] the classroom balance from teacher-directed to student-centered learning."[11]

And although Thomas Good and Jere Brophy do not condemn all lecturing, as long as there is give-and-take and engagement of the audience,[12] they remind us that "classroom experiences also involve learning to become self-reliant and self-evaluative, as well as how to work productively with others."[13]

"Scaffolding" is a term one hears frequently from educators. Good and Brophy define it as "a general term for the task assistance or simplification strategies that teachers might use to bridge the gap between what students are capable of doing on their own and what they are capable of doing with help. . . . Closely associated with the notion of scaffolding is the notion of *gradual transfer of responsibility for managing learning*."[14]

Principal Dave Taylor uses the analogy of a building under construction to explain scaffolding:

It's like if I were building a building, my scaffold's going to start off at a low level to begin with, I'm going to build the building up to that point, then I'll build up higher, then a higher scaffold, then higher, etc., etc. The idea is that, as a teacher, I provide the support that they need to get to a level. If I just say, "You need to be here," and then say, "Get there," students will never get to that level.

It all goes back to Vygotsky's "Zone of Proximal Development." The idea of proximal development is that every person where they are has a certain level that they can attain on their own, and they have a level that they can attain with assistance. That is called their "zone of proximal development."

If you try to approach someone outside of their zone of proximal development, they will shut down, not learn it, and you'll fail. If you go within their zone of proximal development and push them along, their zone expands, and you can then move back and keep going, keep going, keep going. That's the importance of scaffolding. The idea is, "What's within my reach academically? What can I get to?"

For example, my eighteen-month-old sons won't be able to pick up *The Old Man and the Sea* and read it. That's well outside their zone of proximal development. But if we sing the alphabet, when we get to the end they know to clap, because they know that's what we always do at the end of it, so that right there we can use that as a building block for them. So you have to know what can our students do and how do you get them to where you need them to be. Essentially it comes down to breaking things down to the students' level and stretching their learning within that.

"Where they need to be" has now been better clarified by Ohio's acceptance of the Common Core State Standards, which seeks to bring more uniformity to state standards throughout the country. As stated on the Common Core State Standards website, "It should be clear to every student, parent, and teacher what the standards of success are in every school."[15]

The standard for math "*emphasizes mathematical modeling*, the use of mathematics and statistics to analyze empirical situations, understand them and improve decisions."

For example, the draft standards state, "Modeling links classroom mathematics and statistics to everyday life, work, and decision-making. It is the process of choosing and using appropriate mathematics and statistics to analyze empirical situations, to understand them better, and to improve decisions. Quantities and their relationships in physical, economic, public policy, social and everyday situations can be modeled using mathematical and statistical methods. When making mathematical models, technology is valuable for varying assumptions, exploring consequences, and comparing predictions with data." The English standards give examples of literary works appropriate for each grade level.[16]

Attaining those standards is the focus of the curriculum. At DECA, says Dave Taylor, "The way we structure the curriculum is so that we gradually wean the kids off the supports that we provide, and so early on there's a lot of academic support, structure, in the form of 'Here's how it needs to be done.' It's very black and white: 'This is due tomorrow. Sit down and do it. Do it this way and turn it in at this point.' As they get older, we try to scaffold the process between starting high school and actually getting into college, so that when they do leave us and go into college, there's not that big of a leap for them."

The "state content standards" are provided for all the core subject areas: math, English, social studies, history, and science, delineated by grade levels.

"Some of the skills spiral back around, for example, learning how to write a good essay appears across grade levels. You can see that that would be at one level early and be at a more sophisticated level later. It's the backbone of what we do," Judy Hennessey explains. In addition, DECA has prioritized what is called "power standards," calling for higher levels of achievement.

Although the standards are set, DECA teachers have a good deal of autonomy in regard to how they attain them, which is one of the attractions for teaching at DECA, Judy says:

> I believe most teachers go into education because they really enjoy seeing children learn. They like the challenge of trying to figure out how to teach something, and they want to be connected to the kids. But institutionally little by little we have become more mechanized, standardized, unionized, and the offside of that is we have harnessed teachers and really taken away their autonomy in the room, their creativity.
>
> I think that's in part why these teachers stay. No one's telling them how to teach something. They're very clear about what it is we have to teach, and then how to get there is left up to them. I think the more that we restrict that—and even now, I've seen some examples—I've heard people talk about it. Superintendents frequently say, "Well, we give our teachers a script: 'This is how you teach reading. You read this, and the kids do this.'" And I don't think those programs work.
>
> So are there weak teachers who just couldn't perform here? Absolutely, but in general I believe that we recognize teachers are pretty motivated to teach kids to learn, and I've seen that in dozens and dozens of settings, private, public, parochial, and then the other teachers who get to stay who are either incompetent or unmotivated—they can really drag down the morale of a school.

Judy sees her role as that of "the cheerleader. And sometimes the hammer, but the real thinking is done by the teachers. I'm a better organizer, so I can say, for example, 'Let's look at the data. How many of our kids are positioned to pass the Ohio graduation test? Who's iffy, who's marginal?' So when we look at data we can say, 'OK, what should we do?' It's not just the test; they need to know this stuff. And then the teachers become very creative about what to do."

Dave Taylor elaborates:

> The state tells you what you have to teach, so by the end of the year a student has to have x, y, and z complete. As an administrator, I have very little to do with that. In a lot of schools, there is a lot of top-down "here's how you're going to do it." We don't do that here, we really don't. We leave a lot of that up to the teacher and up to the department.
>
> I know when I was teaching at DECA, I built my curriculum based on the content standards, and I was accountable obviously to the principal, but mostly accountable to others in my department. We sat down monthly and we would

go over what it is that we were covering, how we were covering it, how we were assessing it, and how it was going to line up for the next person, so if I'm sending my kids to government class, there are certain things that they've got to have set up from my American history class in order to be successful there.

There's no hiding it. The next year they're going to have government, and the teacher is going to say, "These kids do not understand economics, and you didn't do a good job teaching them the Great Depression, so you should go back over it and cover it more." Those kinds of things we check out in every department.

The manner in which DECA is governed encourages such innovation. The school counts on a stellar group of trustees: leaders in industry, the health field, and education, along with parent representatives. Judy Hennessey explains that

most public-school districts have an elected board. Many times a [public school] board member comes with an agenda, and because they're elected, it seems that it affects their ability to take risks or to encourage innovation, I think, because you don't want to rattle the community too much. But when you have a more corporate board, most of them have become successful by becoming mavericks, and so they're always pushing us to say, "Well, let's not think about the same way we've been doing it. That is possible. Why can't we?"

It changes the way you look at policy, it changes the way you look at your budget, and it certainly changes our day-to-day innovation. If you're fearful that you rock the boat too much, you're really going to maintain the status quo pretty much, but if you're pushed to say, "The only way we're going to get better results is to try something we haven't. What can we try?" it lets us be more creative.

While working toward results, it's also essential to measure how much progress each student is making. In addition to employing the usual tests, Dave Taylor believes it is important to be informed in other ways, too, through nongraded ways of measuring what students know, or "formative assessment":

The principle behind formative assessment is that, rather than waiting until final assessment, or the summative assessment, I'm assessing you all along in small chunks to ensure that you're getting the material, and I will adjust what I'm doing to accommodate you.

This is nothing new. This is not a new science that education has come up with. This has really been around from the beginning, but we educators are placing more of an emphasis on it because there has been so much made of the summative assessments—tests, exams, papers, the things that come at the end—that we're ignoring and not placing as much significance on the shorter-term, intermediate assessments that really help teachers adjust what they're doing.

The whole idea of formative assessment is that it is used both by the student and the teacher to make improvements. A test really isn't always the most clear indicator of what someone knows, and so what you'd use are a variety of means to assess how a student is coming along. That doesn't mean that you can't use a test as a formative assessment—no one's saying that—but if that's your only means, something's wrong. You need to go back and you need to adjust to make sure that you are really gauging what your students know.

For example, a formative assessment can be an exit slip. At the end of the class period, I say to the students, "Before you leave, the way you get out of here is by writing down what is the reason why the United States got involved in World War II," if that was our lesson for the day. The students could write that out, give it to me, then I can look at it very quickly and see, "OK, these fifteen kids got it, these six kids didn't. I need to talk to these six kids tomorrow and make sure that we get that."

The whole point is there are very, very quick ways to do this. Usually a test—you administer it, grade it: "You were wrong." You don't always go back, reteach, regroup, and make sure that students have gotten it.

Students, too, can check their progress by checking the data available on each student through the Management Analysis Network ("MAN"), a DECA innovation that we'll hear more about later.

NOTES

1. Edward T. Hall, *Beyond Culture* (New York: Anchor, 1989), 208.
2. Hall, *Beyond Culture*, 205.
3. Hall, *Beyond Culture*, 205.
4. Quoted in Thomas J. Lasley II, Thomas J. Matczynski, and James B. Rowley, *Instructional Models: Strategies for Teaching in a Diverse Society*, 2nd ed. (Belmont, CA: Wadsworth/Thomson Learning, 2002), 10.
5. Harvard Graduate School of Education/Jobs for the Future, "Summary of Preliminary Findings," *Early College High School Study*, June 18, 2004, 3.
6. Lasley, Matczynski, and Rowley, *Instructional Models*, 11–12.
7. Lasley, Matczynski, and Rowley, 44.
8. Allan C. Ornstein and Thomas J. Lasley II, *Strategies for Effective Teaching*, 4th ed. (Boston: McGraw Hill, 2004), 8.
9. Ornstein and Lasley, *Strategies for Effective Teaching*, 10.
10. Steven Zemelman, Harvey Daniels, and Arthur Hyde, *Best Practice: Today's Standards for Teaching and Learning in America's Schools* (Portsmouth, NH: Heinemann, 2005), 227.
11. Zemelman, Daniels, and Hyde, *Best Practice*, 228.
12. Thomas L. Good and Jere E. Brophy, *Looking in Classrooms*, 8th ed. (New York: Addison-Wesley, 2000), 382.
13. Good and Brophy, *Looking in Classrooms*, 17–18.
14. Good and Brophy, *Looking in Classrooms*, 424.
15. Common Core State Standards Initiative, www.corestandards.org/the-standards.
16. Common Core State Standards Initiative.

Chapter Nine

Raising the Bar

DECA's "what we have to teach" is another factor that differentiates it from traditional high schools, for it is geared to sending every graduate to college, and, more importantly, giving them the skills to stay there and graduate; it is much harder to keep urban kids in college than it is to get them there. Among the thirty-four countries belonging to the Organisation for Economic Co-operation and Development, the United States ranks eighth in college enrollment, but second to last in graduation. [1]

DECA, however, is bucking the trend, with its 84 percent college-graduation rate. It helps that the scaffolding is put in place so that there is not too much "culture shock" when the graduates enter college, and that students are required to take college classes while still in high school.

From the moment the students walk in the door, the goal of college is very much in the forefront, as demonstrated by the attention given to the ACT, the standardized test that measures high-school achievement, commonly used for college admissions. As Kanika Jones points out:

> If you walk around, you'll see posters all over the place, they're pink, yellow, and red, black and white, and they'll say "ACT Quality Core Standards." They'll show you something like, "If you focus on these standards, this is the score that you'll probably get." We have them broken down by grade level, as well.

A long hallway is filled with the smiling photographs of DECA alumni with the names of the colleges they are attending, and college letters of acceptance are prominently displayed when they're received.

Future lawyer LaTonya is happy to have the exposure to college that she would not get in another school. She explains that because we are a college-preparatory school, it would be appropriate to make sure that the high-school students know what college feels like. You have the high-school aspect as well, but you also know what a college feels like, because you are taking classes and also multitasking for a job, internship, job shadows, community service, and things like that. [Taking college classes now] actually does give me a lot of confidence. . . . It feels good to know that my classmates there aren't underestimating me because I'm in high school.

DECA is performance-based, rather than time-based, as with the traditional Carnegie unit requirements; a handout assures parents and others that the school is "results oriented; no social promotion." Although most students complete the program in four years, some have finished in three years, others take longer than four.

In addition to a curriculum tied to content standards, DECA has created an overlay of college classes, plus independent work. "The guiding principle," says Judy Hennessey,

is that it will allow DECA to embed the college-going behavior as requirements. I'll give you several examples: it is not optional here to go on college visits, to take the ACT twice, not once but twice, to take a prep course, to apply for scholarships, to complete your applications to a "reach" school and a guaranteed school. Those are all embedded in these performance milestones, and that gives us leverage with students and parents. In a lot of urban high schools, only a fraction of the kids take the ACT, so they don't know whether they're ready for college or not. They just don't take the test.

Here we start a college plan as soon as they come into the ninth grade, and so all of those things that middle- and upper-income parents do for their children, we try to make as requirements. That guides our instruction as well, and in the end we look at the ACT standards, and we refer to a really nice research study called *College Knowledge*. They interviewed literally thousands of university admissions and freshman professors to find out what they expected of incoming college students, and they pulled it together in the book *College Knowledge*.

If you look on some of our walls in the school corridors, you'll see the ACT laid out. What do you have to do to get a score of 28? What do you have to do to get a 24? It's very clear.

So that's our reference point, and I'll give you another example of where that really helps us. We learned that a three- to five-page cogent paper that has a thesis, supporting citations, and a good summary is a deal-breaker in college, so we just hammer the three- to five-page paper.

Every time you turn around here, you are writing a three- to five-page paper—when you do community service, when you do a job shadow, when you do your internship, when you answer questions on an exam, we are just [doing this] over and over, so at least we know that that skill is in hand for the kids.

And we get really good feedback about that. The kids say when they get to college, a lot of the kids don't know how to put a paper together, and they do.

When I see some of their writing, though, I just shake my head, because the mechanics are not great, that's for sure. We have a lot of kids who don't know parts of speech, they don't have the foundation. So that's how we decide what to teach. We take those content standards, we assign them to certain courses, we take the power ones, or the ones we drive home, and then we have this overview of what they are going to do on the "gatekeeper" tests.

In spite of the time and effort required, sooner or later students come to appreciate what they have gained at DECA, students like Bryson, who recognizes that the urban poor often "don't have the tools to teach their children what they need to know, so from birth it's kind of like a setback." He says:

When I talk to people about our school, I truly say that DECA is a school of transformation, because it takes these students who are not expected to succeed and gives them the tools and forces them to succeed, and they will come back to the community in the end and benefit the community.

First of all, showing them how to work hard. Giving them things that they need to be successful. Not just being all A students, but giving them the tools: being able to study effectively, effective test-taking skills, how to network, how to be professional when you're speaking to a group of people. Tools like that, not just are they the best in math, reading, and writing. A lot of them aren't, but learning how to think—that's the most important tool—teaching them how to think effectively.

With the heavy attention given to study, "Nerd Nights" have become a DECA tradition. Held on a Friday night before the end of each semester, Nerd Night consists of three hours of study after school, followed by a party. Parents, students, and often teachers bring refreshments, and the games and dancing go on until 11:00 p.m.

As one staff member explains,

My kids go to [an affluent suburban school], and they would be like, "Forget it. We're just going to stay home and study," but our kids, our population here, enjoy being at school. It's an easier place for many of them to do work, it's an easier place for many of them to have fun.

We also have study tables, I think three times a week, and it's amazing how many students will attend it, because for a lot of them it's an easier environment to get homework done in than going home is.

Central to the DECA system are the "Gateways," six challenging packages of requirements that become progressively more difficult, and a good deal of time in advisory periods is spent on preparing for them. In addition to regular classroom instruction, Gateways require completion of more than a hundred community service hours, two professional job internships, three job shadows, a twenty-page autobiography, three college courses, five in-depth research projects, twenty-one literary analysis papers, and a 95 percent attendance rate. A handbook spells out specific requirements for each Gateway, with detailed criteria for each segment.

Presenting a Gateway has been compared to being on trial in a court of law, or to the opening night of a Broadway show; it's high drama. Students must argue their case before a panel of teachers, parents, other students, a member of the board of trustees, and notable outside visitors. With the aid of PowerPoint presentations, they must prove that they have successfully accomplished the Gateway requirements, responding to probing questions from the panel. Passing a Gateway is a cause for celebration, analogous to passing a grade.

Sometimes, Jolena says,

> The kids complain, "Oh, Gateway work is too much work," but when we hear [graduates] say that Gateway work helped prepare them for college and put them ahead of everyone else in college, that gives us some kind of positive affirmation that it's a good thing for us; it's a good thing to do.
>
> Gateways are really to prepare you for college, because you're doing above and beyond, like you're doing papers, analyzing, presenting exhibitions that prepare you for the application that you'll have to do in the real world: explaining the concept, and mastering that concept, being able to articulate it for other people, community service—which gets you involved with your community and giving back—and other things of that nature: job shadows, internships, which are not typical things required at traditional schools. It's not just high school; they're preparing you for college and after college your career and your work life.

As director of community involvement, Anne Rasmussen has a great deal to do with that preparation, coordinating the job shadows, internships, and community service required for the Gateways, all of which have received an "incredibly positive response" from the community.

Anne explains that a job shadow is a one-day opportunity, to see, for example, "what it's like to be in a law firm, or see what it's like to be in engineering offices, or see what it's like to be a nurse." A written "reflection" of the experience is required.

Students must write a more demanding three- to five-page paper with a thoughtful analysis following internships, which are much more extended. Forty hours of active time must be spent with an organization, time that can be divided up in different ways, perhaps one afternoon a week for ten weeks, or eight hours for five days during the summer.

The student's participation varies from place to place, she says:

> It depends on what kind of work the student is being exposed to, but primarily it's extended observation, and we make sure that the businesses understand that, for there's obviously a big difference between a sophomore or junior in

high school and a junior in college in terms of the skill set that they're going to come in with and the maturity level, and that kind of thing.

Our kids will end up working on little projects sometimes, but mostly it's just an opportunity to maybe shadow a variety of people within a company, so that each time they visit they might be with a different person or a different department so that they can get a better understanding of how the whole organization works.

I had a girl who just recently did an internship with an accounting firm. The accountant was worried that she was going to be bored to tears, the student was a little worried that it was going to be boring, and it was anything but. There was just enough diversity in what the accountant planned for her experience and there was enough professionalism that I think she found it to be really cool!—to be around adults doing real business and talking about real money and seeing the challenges of that.

She saw the accountant just come unglued one day when one of his clients was furious about something, and she came away from that day saying, "Oh my gosh, Miss R, he got all mad because this woman was yelling at him!"

Stuff like that happens in life, and then he talked about how you get through that and had a whole conversation with her about when you have an angry or upset client and how you deal with that kind of thing. So even in the world of numbers, it can still be dynamic and interesting on a level that a high school student can understand and connect with.

She was with the person who owned the company. He took her to client meetings, he took her to professional meetings, and he took her to training sessions that his staff was having, so she had exposure to all this. She was not really asked to perform, but he made sure that he thought through what days would be the most meaningful for her, so instead of saying, "You'll come every single Tuesday for two months," he would customize the days, based on when he thought something interesting that she would learn from would happen.

That's the kind of custom internship that I aspire to as much as possible: to get the partnership organization to think it through, to think about what kind of things would trigger the interests of a high school student and then customize it so that the student comes on specific days and goes to specific events and meetings, and that kind of thing.

What I like to see with these internships is that our kids get some exposure to possible jobs in the real world that they could actually have. It starts the networking process for them, so while they're still in high school they know someone right here who works at an engineering firm, and they've spent ten weeks with those people.

Even if it doesn't end up that they directly get a college internship or a summer job or something out of it, they've at least got the person's business card, there's a little history, they can call upon the people they worked with just possibly to give them other ideas on where they could get summer work or get an internship or for when they get out of college. This is what I try to keep in the forefront of my mind as I make these connections for our students.

I don't want them to just think they're going on a theoretical internship; I will look at what they've done to start: "I will now spend ten weeks with a nurse," for example. I want them to think of this as the beginning of the pipeline for themselves, and I want our community partners—these businesses and organizations—to start thinking of it that way as well.

When it's done really well—most of the time I like to think it's done pretty darn well—I think most of our kids are pleasantly surprised and their eyes are often opened in a way they don't even expect. They say they had no idea that such and such was like that: "I had no idea that's what being a lawyer is really like. I thought maybe they were in court all the time."

The students are aspiring to professional positions, but their families typically are working class, so there's nobody to go home to and hear the stories of Mom's day as a doctor, or Dad's day as an engineer or an accountant or whatever.

The other thing that I think our kids really enjoy is that most of the people who want to do this with our students have a terrific attitude with our kids. They are professional people, they understand the values of these ideas, and they see what this could do for the students' self-confidence, so rarely are our students put in a position where someone is patronizing.

With the help of the Rotary Club, Anne also coordinates an annual career fair that introduces students to those in various professions. A monthly speakers series is presented by Premier Health Partners, "another way to bring the community to the students," and one that often features speakers whose road to success was not easy.

One of Anne Rasmussen's more challenging, but gratifying, responsibilities is teaching the corporate etiquette class to ninth-grade students. "That's pretty early in their high-school career to be exposed to some of these ideas," she says, "but because we have to get them ready for jobs shadows and internships, we need to present this information to them fairly early on."

At the end of the quarter-long class there is a corporate etiquette luncheon in celebration at the University of Dayton with invited guests, for which everyone has to dress up. She explains that there has been a "dry-run of dining etiquette expectations so they can be comfortable in a professional situation where they've got to eat out. We have a very formal luncheon with conversation that's at a professional level, and it's fun."

During the course of the class, she says,

We talk about how to write professionally, how to write a thank-you note, how to write a professional e-mail, how to give a professional oral presentation. What does it mean to have good body language? Why is body language important? Why is it important to think about how you're dressing? I try to introduce the kids to the idea that there are cultural norms that they're just going to have to understand and accept.

As much as you want to rebel against it at age fifteen, if you want to be involved with these groups of people that you're think you're aspiring to be involved with, then they make the rules. And if you want to be a banker, you're probably going to wear a suit. If you want to work for a graphic design firm, you'll probably get to wear jeans, and everything in between.

We talk about language. How good grammar is important. How slang is not very acceptable. Why speaking with the best vocabulary is really important, and what that shows about who you are. Why work ethic is important.

Something I keep reading about, so I've introduced these terms to the kids, is the idea about hard and soft skills. Hard skills are things like knowing how to use a computer, knowing how to take blood pressure if you're a nurse, knowing how to perform surgery—but soft skills are things like knowing to show up for work on time, knowing to be polite, knowing that it's important to do your best work, knowing to be self-motivated, knowing how to be a problem solver, being conscientious—all these things are soft skills.

What most people in the professional world are saying is you can hire people who are perfectly trained in their hard skills, and they will lose their jobs because they lack soft skills, that they don't understand, for example, that if you're told to be at work at 8:00 and they keep showing up at 8:20, that that's a problem.

For a lot of our kids that does not come naturally. The culture that they've come from allows for the breakdown of many soft skills. Many of the dining etiquette ideas are soft skills. And our kids are like, "That's not how we eat at our house. I just grab a bite and go to my room." So the idea of setting a table, sitting together and having a conversation—these are often new ideas for a lot of our kids.

It is the teaching of such skills that Thomas Friedman notes is one attribute of successful schools, according to an international study. Such schools "are data-driven and transparent, not only around learning outcomes, but also around soft skills like completing work on time, resilience, perseverance—and punctuality."[2]

Students must thus adapt to "code-switching," matching their demeanor to the circumstances. When it comes to the Gateways as well, they must dress professionally, and also speak professionally, before the audience of teachers, staff, and parents. It's not unknown for a student to be turned away from a Gateway presentation and told to return in proper attire.

Jolena tells me that "sometimes there are fashion shows to show the students how to dress and how not to dress, which is a very good way to make it entertaining, but also make it informative, which I think is a really good idea and I think that works a lot."

"Here at DECA," says Kaneesha,

we have to work on our presenting skills. To help us with our presenting skills for our Gateways, we have to do exhibitions, for which we have to write up a research paper and create a PowerPoint on it, and then we have to present in front of the teacher. If you want, students can come in and listen. During the presentation you have to know how to speak and say the correct things, instead of talking informally, in slang.

To me Gateways are different challenges to get you prepared for college. You have to do about four book reflections where you give a summary. You

have to write how you relate to the book, plus there are the community service
hours and the job shadows and internships.

Bryson can appreciate the college preparation he is receiving compared to
students at other places, since "a lot of my family go to different schools. I do
a lot of community service at [other high schools], and you can visibly see
the differences. Like our first year we were brought up on PowerPoints and
how to correctly do a paper, but a lot of students in their senior year at other
schools couldn't tell you how to do PowerPoint or how to do papers. I felt
bad for them. How can you expect them to compete with the other students if
they're already this far behind?"

Presentations can be on a variety of things. While Kaneesha's most recent
one focused on evolution, Andre, whose young niece had Down Syndrome,
presented on awareness of that congenital condition. He has also given presentations on the planets, explaining why Pluto isn't a planet anymore, and on
steam engines. Damarion, who plans to be a doctor, has presented on arterio-
sclerosis and how it can be prevented with aggressive statin treatment and
life changes.

In addition to experience in public speaking at the Gateways, there are
other opportunities for gaining confidence in front of an audience. As Bryson
says, "Dr. Hennessey will put you on the spot when visitors come in and tell
you to speak in front of them. So in order to keep from looking stupid in front
of them, you have to figure out how to sound professional, to shake hands,
make eye contact. She grooms us for this." Although at home students may
speak informally in the style they're used to, "the teachers basically teach
you how to be a chameleon, how to switch atmospheres, so when we're in a
professional setting, use your professional voice," he says.

The advisors, too, "really instill in us using correct grammar, greeting
people appropriately, and making sure we conduct and carry ourselves in a
professional manner," says Damarion. "DECA gives you some really good
life skills."

Those like Bryson who choose to be DECA Ambassadors get even more
experience: "We're the people who rally on behalf of the school. We talk to a
lot of entrepreneurs, businessmen, other schools. We pretty much have visitors here every week, sometimes two or three times a week, and Dr. Hennessey pulls the student Ambassadors out to show them. She says, 'DECA is
great. I want you to hear from the students, because I could talk to you all
day, but when you hear it from the students, it's a totally new experience.'"

While community service stresses the importance of giving back, job
shadows and internships offer students exposure to a world they might otherwise not know. LaTonya, for example, from an early age would tell her
mother, "You know, Mom, I want to be a lawyer." She says, "It was like 'I
want to be a lawyer, but I don't know what that involves.' I was able to job

shadow a wonderful lawyer, and she really sparked my desire to be a lawyer even more. It was a wonderful thing because it made me realize, 'OK, I really want to be a defense attorney.' I have to be a defense attorney. There's no other thing that I can be!"

Keneesha thinks that the best things about DECA are "the job shadows, community service, and internships, because you actually get to go out and help the communities, with the job shadows you get to watch whatever field you want to work in, and with the internships, instead of just going out and watching, you get to interact in the field that you want to work in. As for me, I want to be a zoologist, so when I took my dog to the vet, I job shadowed there for a day," she says.

Enthusiastic Jewanna, who hopes to be a biomedical engineer, job-shadowed "very helpful" nurses in the neonatal unit, burn unit, cardiac unit, and orthopedic unit at a large hospital. She also spent a week participating in a program for women engineers at the University of Dayton.

Damarion, the future physician, balked, however, at doing any internship at all—"just one of those teen things, where you don't want to give up your summer to go back to school." But, he says, "I ended up loving the internship, actually, so that was a big plus for me. We learned different subjects about medicine, did various labs—we actually got to work with real cadavers—learned about different parts. It was very interesting. I was intrigued by it."

One very practical reason for such outside experience is to help the students determine their majors in college, for they can't afford to keep switching majors and thus extend their university years. Another result of such programs is that students no longer fear approaching the experts for advice. Mentors are an important part of students' lives in helping them prepare for a better life. It was future doctor Damarion's mentor who persuaded the reluctant student to enter a medicine-oriented internship.

For Andre, whose close family members have suffered from drug addiction, it has been a great uncle who is also his pastor who has been his mentor and with whom he is "very close." He and his great aunt "have been a huge influence on my life, and the pastor—he works at the [Air Force] Base, actually—so he's successful, he always pushes me to do better in school. He's always telling me, 'You can do anything that you put your mind to. Never let what your family does affect you; the choices they made, you don't have to make.' He always makes it clear that my life is my life."

Daron has been living with his suburban white mentors since his father expelled him from the house after a "very, very, very big misunderstanding and disagreement." The future politician, who with his height and build looks more like a football pro than the scholar he is, says he was always intellectually inclined and "spoke differently" from the rest of the family. Now it seems as though this bookish "ugly duckling" has finally found his place among scholarly swans. One of the best things about living with his young white mentors, he says, is:

> the abundance of knowledge they have. They know so much that I can ask almost any kind of question, and they would be able to answer it. And the best part about it is they've been through the college process. . . .
>
> At first I thought, "Wow! They're really smarter than me," but when I expressed that to them, they said, "Now, don't feel like you're inferior to us, because we're all equal. You know things that we don't know." They said, "We're not government people, so we would ask *you* government questions," but anything pertaining to math, science—my [new mom] was an English major, so writing—they could cover everything except social studies.
>
> And it makes the pieces of the puzzle fit so well, because I'm very good at social studies. I'm not good at math, I'm not good at science, and I'm OK at English and language arts, so all of our knowledge together creates a pool, an abundance of knowledge.

When it appeared that the scholarship that Daron had been awarded would not cover his tuition and other expenses at his expensive university, his mentors were instrumental in finding him an additional special scholarship for disadvantaged youth.

A Harvard study in 2004 indicated the place that mentors hold at DECA: "We asked whether students had a mentor either at school or outside of school, and we found that . . . more than half of DECA students had a mentor. . . . This likely speaks to the built-in advising function at DECA."[3]

Mentors can indeed make all the difference. In his bestselling *The Other Wes Moore*, the author Wes Moore, former Rhodes scholar and successful businessman, wrote of a man of the same name whose background had been very similar to his, but who had ended up serving a lifetime sentence in prison. A demanding education and a series of mentors, especially in the military, led to one's success, while the other remains in prison.[4]

DECA students have learned to have no hesitation about asking for help when they need it. While visiting Washington with a small group, Daron ran across a well-known CNN anchorman in a restaurant. He amazed his classmates by returning to the table with the celebrity's card, cell phone number, and the promise of a future internship when he attends American University!

Acting as role models, too, are the many volunteers, often community leaders, who tutor, facilitate book discussion groups, edit student papers, invite students to participate in community events, or offer their services in other ways. Among them is Ohio's former governor Bob Taft, who teaches at the University of Dayton. Each year he conducts a seminar at DECA on a subject of vital interest. Last year's focused on community revitalization, this year's on immigration.

Although college thoughts are always looming in the background, it is Danya Berry, the college liaison staff member, whose job it is to turn those dreams into a reality. "She has an amazing ability to connect with the kids," Judy Hennessey says. "She's the one who works with the kids on all their applications. She registers them for their Sinclair [Community College] classes. She's the parent *in loco parentis*, really. Without her the kids would not get their college applications in."

When Judy Hennessey worked in an affluent suburb in which most of the parents were college graduates, she would say,

> "You need to have this paperwork in, because if you want to be considered for admission, let's get it in five days early." That doesn't work here. You have to say, "OK, go sit over there and get this part done." And call the parent, and then you have to say, "Tomorrow morning bring this part."
>
> It is so much staging, I guess. "Scaffolding" is the term we often use in education. So you take it incrementally, and she has a gift. I mean, she's just really good at not annoying the kids, because they can resist and get nothing done. And working with the families on some very private information. They stay in touch with her, as well as with the advisors. We know a lot about our kids, and they come back.

Mrs. Berry's job entails more than just seeing that a student gets in college. According to Dave Taylor, "She keeps track of where all the students are, what they're up to. Right now if I want to know, 'Where's so-and-so?' she'll tell you where they are, how they're doing, and she can give you a working phone number for them. She does a good job of staying up with them."

* * *

But why earn college credits in high school? The Early College High School Initiative's website explains that such a program "is a bold approach, based on the principle that academic rigor, combined with the opportunity to save time and money, is a powerful motivator for students to work hard and meet intellectual challenges. Early college high schools blend high school and college in a rigorous yet supportive program, compressing the time it takes to complete a high school diploma and the first two years of college."

The purpose of the Initiative, begun in 2002 primarily with the help of the Gates Foundation, has been to remedy the statistics at that time, according to which "for nearly 100 low-income students who start high school, only 65 will get a high school diploma and only 45 will enroll in college. Only 11 will complete a postsecondary degree." In what the Initiative called America's nine hundred to one thousand urban "dropout factories," only half the students will graduate.

And the Early College High Schools are showing results. By 2007, 75 percent of the more than nine hundred graduates of seventeen such schools had been accepted to four-year colleges, while others had chosen to complete an Associate's degree by spending a fifth year at their high schools and taking additional college courses. More than 85 percent had received "substantial college credit." Learning "takes place in small learning environments that demand rigorous, high-quality work and provide extensive support," support that is social, as well as academic. [5]

According to a Harvard report, "the ECHS [Early College High School] experience reflects a new contract with learning, facilitated in part through the crafting of a different type of relationship with teachers, one that is highly relational in nature, kindles interest in future possibility development, and supports engagement along pathways leading toward those possible future goals. It is a relationship in which students describe learning as 'fun,' because it is interactive, cooperative, relevant, and culturally responsive to their lives." [6]

"I am proud to say that I attend an innovative early college academy," Dannisha says, "not because my future is guaranteed, but because I can choose to have one."

NOTES

1. Paul Tough, *How Children Succeed: Grit, Curiosity, and the Hidden Power of Character* (New York: Houghton Mifflin Harcourt, 2012), 150.

2. Thomas L. Friedman, "My Little (Global) School," *New York Times*, April 3, 3013.

3. Harvard Graduate School of Education/Jobs for the Future, "Preliminary Quantitative Findings," December 2004, 2.

4. Wes Moore, *The Other Wes Moore: One Name, Two Fates* (New York: Spiegel and Grau, 2010).

5. Early College High School Initiative, "Overview & FAQ," www.earlycolleges.org/overview.html.

6. Karen C. Foster and Michael Nakkula, *Early College High School: Igniting and Sustaining Educational Identity Development*, Harvard Graduate School of Education Risk and Prevention Program, December 7, 2004, 14.

Chapter Ten

Bumps in the Road

Although the school now serves as a model for those who would emulate its success, it wasn't smooth sailing in the beginning. Although the basic plans seemed sound, implementing them would prove to be a challenge.

DECA was born in 2003 through the efforts of the Dayton Public Schools, the Gates Foundation, the Knowledge Works Foundation, and others, under the leadership of Dr. Thomas Lasley II, then dean of education at the University of Dayton, a private Catholic institution.

Well before that time, however, according to Judy Hennessey:

> The Bill and Melinda Gates Foundation had been doing research on the deplorable status of urban high schools, and they had come to a lot of conclusions. Most of the schools were too big, they were dysfunctional as institutions, there were low expectations, the kids weren't exposed to the kind of academics they were going to need, nobody talked about college. As in the movie *Waiting for "Superman,"* there was the notion of "We're doing a really good job producing dropouts."
>
> So they approached the then new president of the University of Dayton, Dan Curran, through Tom Lasley. Percy Mack was a brand new superintendent in Dayton, charter enrollment was growing, and the district wanted some other options for their high school students. The timing was right, and actually Tom Lasley really championed getting it started, so we were the first in Ohio.
>
> Now, the Gates people, through an intermediary called Knowledge Works, had planned to seed more. It wasn't going to be just DECA in Ohio but they got this one off the ground hurriedly. They decided to do it, I believe finally in the November, December range, and by August the school was open.
>
> Then within a short period of time, about six years, there were nine early college high schools in Ohio. At the same time the Gates people were seeding these in other states. Texas has a huge network, North Carolina had started to make it a statewide initiative, Utah had some counseling.

117

> Now there are more than two hundred of these across the country. Early college high schools are different in how they're set up, but they all have this [thinking that] kids go to college while they're in high school. They at least get a taste of it.

Tom Lasley recalls that "the Gates Foundation was working through a regional foundation, and the Gates money came to us through Knowledge Works." Tom would serve as the first president of the board of trustees.

At first classes were held on the University of Dayton campus, which was not without its difficulties. Since the university is a Catholic institution, some university leaders felt that it was inappropriate for it to "operate a public high school, especially when local Catholic schools were closing themselves for lack of students."[1]

Space was also a problem for the beginning class of a hundred or so students. Tom Lasley remembers that "the first year we didn't have any building, so we were kind of all over the campus. It was a mess. We were everywhere, wherever we could find some empty space," which came to interfere with other campus activities, especially when the volleyball coach wanted them out of the gym when practices started. Eventually DECA would find a home on the third floor of a university-owned building on the edge of campus.

DECA began, not as a charter school, but rather as a "sort of hybrid, a district contract school,"[2] although it would become a charter in 2007. That was when the school levy for the city of Dayton failed to pass; teachers would have to be laid off for lack of funds. Union rules decreed that the most junior of teachers, those young, enthusiastic teachers who were the best on DECA's staff, would have to leave. And so DECA became a charter school with the Dayton Public Schools as its sponsor.

Charter schools, as Steven Brill defines them, are

> publicly financed and open to any child, but they are run by entities other than the conventional school district. Typically, they are operated by nonprofit organizations that rely on donations to provide seed money to launch the school but then use the same amount, or less tax money per pupil, as is doled out to the public schools for ongoing operations. Those who run charter schools are accountable for the school's performance. However, they are free to manage as they wish, which includes the freedom to hire teachers who are not union members.[3]

Terry Ryan of the Fordham Foundation remembers the trials of DECA's beginnings. As with any new enterprise, there were times when it was touch and go, especially when DECA chose to opt out of the district. During what Terry calls the school's "near-death experience," there were obstacles to overcome—politically, operationally, and financially.

At one time the teachers' union attempted to sue Tom Lasley to prevent the school's leaving the district, he says, but with the help of then state senator Jon Husted and others, it was able to become a charter. If the school had remained in the district, Terry avers, it would have meant its death knell, for DECA would have had no say in which teachers were assigned there, thus losing the "fantastic culture" that makes it so effective.

"We need more schools like DECA," he says, "and to get there we need to open the human talent pipeline so that our best and brightest will work in schools like DECA."

There would be other changes over the years. DECA's first principal was Tim Nealon, the retired principal of Stivers School for the Arts, one of the city's better high schools, who had moved out of state. He agreed to come back to Dayton "but not for very long" to get the school started. Tim was a "warm, charismatic" person, says Judy Hennessey, who "put some wonderful things in place—the advisories, having performance-based evaluation, reaching out to the community to try to get kids in the community—and Mr. Nealon was the right person to convince parents to send their children to a school when they didn't even know how they were going to graduate them."

Tom Lasley remembers those early days, too. "The idea of the advisories has evolved, but the early notion was to create a connection, an emotional connection between each teacher with the students. You know," he admits, "it's like everything, at first it was probably a little bit too loosey-goosey, and then it was probably not defined very well initially. But over time it's gotten more and more refined. Tim was there a year and a half, and then Judy came."

With the arrival of Judy Hennessey in December 2004, the school was in for some changes, and not all of them were welcome. "Tim had been in the Dayton public schools," Tom says, "and clearly what he was creating was better than what he thought he had seen. Judy was in the [affluent] Oakwood schools, and when she came in, she thought it was weaker than what she had seen. So I think Judy upped the ante."

She remembers the challenges she faced in her first year:

Oh, my God, they all hated me when I came here. They hated me! I tell you, after about a week here I went home one night and I said, "What have I gotten myself into?" What I saw was way too permissive, not enough structure for teenagers, particularly our kids. I didn't see a lot of great teaching, in fact I saw very little actual teaching. I didn't think they were getting much done. I soon began to understand that if there weren't radical changes, this place would implode. It was such a rough first year. I decided, "Well, I'm not going to have any friends, so I'd better get started on something."

Let me give you an example of that, the OGT [Ohio Graduation Tests]. I came at the end of December, officially at the beginning in January. Nobody knew who was going to take the OGT in March. There was no waiver from the state, nobody was preparing, nobody even knew. And parents thought, "If my kid has been here—if this is their second year, they're going to take the test." And I knew if they took the test, they were so poorly prepared that it would kill us in the media. And our faculty was very divided on it, some saying everybody ought to get as many chances as possible, and some saying they're not ready. I immediately stepped into that hornets' nest.

Well, we got a waiver from the state department that we would base it on the Gateways. And that you had to finish Gateway Two, which bought us some time, and then we started Saturday and Sunday prep sessions, and I mean, we were here late—because we only had a few months by then, like six weeks, to get them ready.

In traditional schools they take it in the spring of their sophomore year. Period. And then you keep taking it either fall or spring until you pass it. You can take it in the summer, but you aren't required to. Well, we based it on our performance requirements, so our kids can take it if they finish Gateway Two in their freshman year, or they might not get to take it until they're a sophomore, depending on how they move through that.

But that was such a hornets' nest right off the bat. . . . That first year there were some people who left, and I certainly didn't mourn their leaving. Now looking back, I probably needed a softer touch.

They were spending money without any—it was like writing checks without any balance, and that's not an overstatement. We were $350,000 in the hole after a year and a half of operation, so I just have to say that looking back, I wouldn't want to have to relive that at all.

And now I would say, I consider these people a second family, and I think they know I would go to bat for them, but at the same time the kids have to know there's an authority figure. You cannot be—all teenagers—you cannot be their friends. You just can't. You're going to say no and you're going to mean it, and they're not going to like it and they're going to whine and stamp their feet and all the other things. But I didn't think the kids had the underlying skills to do all that independent research. They couldn't write a paragraph, let alone put together a paper that they had researched independently.

The tough measures worked. By 2009, DECA had become one of the top-performing high schools in the city. The honors began to accumulate: *U.S. News and World Report*'s bronze medal in 2009 as one of America's Best High Schools, selection as one of five programs in the country named "most innovative" in a study by WestEd for the Bill and Melinda Gates Foundation, the 2009 Urban Impact Award by the Council of Great Cities' Schools, and, for the 2010–2011 school year, a rating of "excellent with distinction" on the Ohio State Report Card. DECA is currently featured on the U.S. Department of Education's website as a "What Works" in secondary reform.

There were other changes over time, too. As Judy reports:

The original benchmark that the Gates people set was that 60 percent of the students would graduate with both a high school diploma and an associate's degree. Now we've had seven do that, but we've backed off that goal. One, it's unrealistic for some of our kids, and two, we don't want to sacrifice their high school experience and curriculum by sending them to college courses ill prepared, so we say at minimum they have to have three college classes under their belt, which is usually nine to twelve hours. Our average is higher than that, but given the fact that we have a first-come, first-served enrollment, it makes it harder for us to get them into more college classes than a handful.

For Principal Dave Taylor, there are always new challenges, new goals. In the coming year he will be working on improving relations between teachers and students and between students and students, as well as formative assessments. Each class, like each student, has a different personality. The coming year's class is not quite so engaged as previous ones, and, he says:

> I think there's been a perception lapse. What I mean by that is that I think that the teachers have assumed that the students were more engaged with them than they actually were. Our data show that. We administer a survey to the students and ask them what their thoughts are about the school, and we just found that we were down in just about every area this year. It's obviously a cause for concern. It's still better than most schools, I'll be honest with you in that way, but we have to seek significant improvement.
>
> So how do we do that? A lot of that is simple things. When the students enter the classroom, smile, greet them at the door, greet them by name. Those are the most common things that students ask for. We're actually conducting a focus group, I'm actually doing that later on this week, and I'm going to ask them questions: Here's what the data say. For example, the first question here is, "Is your school a warm and welcome place?" Is DECA warm and welcoming? What's friendly about it? And what's not? From there we can look at those issues and address and change those things.
>
> Obviously not everything's going to change based on what the kids say, but certainly we can make some significant changes based on what they perceive to be issues. Their perspective is drastically different from ours and for us to look at it and assume that we know what concerns them is short-sighted, especially if we haven't asked them. Maybe you just spend some time hanging out with them at the beginning of the year, but really building relationships with the students.

In spite of the problems, the school continues to be extraordinarily successful. The latest data reveal that it is just slightly below the affluent suburban school districts of Centerville and Oakwood in reading skills; as mentioned, it has been designated "excellent with distinction" by the state of Ohio, and virtually all of its students go to college.

According to the National Student Clearinghouse, 84 percent of DECA alumni are getting their college degrees, placing the school well above other college-graduation rates: 13 percent for graduates of the Dayton Public Schools, 24.6 percent of high school graduates in Ohio, and 28.2 percent in the nation as a whole.[4] The scaffolding kind of support that Dave Taylor describes is paying off. With 73.7 percent of the students at the poverty level, and 87 percent the first in their family to go to college, "We are really defying the odds," says Judy Hennessey. All at school costs per pupil of $9,064, compared to the public school cost of $14,256.

Because many schools are "nonselective," say Abigail and Stephan Thernstrom, "the doors to college are open, even to those with weak academic records. The problem is not getting in but staying and graduating." They cite a study that indicates that three-fourths of the white students entered college, but only 36 percent earned a four-year degree, while three-fourths of the black population studied entered college, but only one in six finished.[5] "Because black students were typically less well prepared academically, they had a much harder time surviving the four years," as did white students who were also poorly prepared.[6]

DECA is also a demonstration site for the *My Voice* © survey, so longitudinal data are available. The survey is offered to all Ohio school districts in 2012 as part of Race to the Top. Judy has found it to be "the best instrument we've run into to try and assess how the student feels about the teacher. Is the work challenging? Does the teacher know when the child's not there? How do parents feel about the education that the child is getting? We track this data by cohort group, we disaggregate it by boy and girl, so we can look at the trends."

Nevertheless, there are still challenges to face. The male-female ratio, for example, is not ideal: close to 68 percent female, which is "not good for the school," Judy says. Nor are ACT results where she would like them to be, even though DECA's results "certainly put us in the elite top 3 percent nationally for urban schools."

Although DECA met sixteen of the state standards, it did not meet that for eighth-grade science, the school having taken a "calculated risk" in adding the seventh and eighth grades in 2007. It was anticipated that DECA would drop from excellent to effective, which did happen for a year, but that score is quickly improving. This year DECA will be implementing a three-year STEM (Science, Technology, Engineering, and Mathematics) phase, doubling up on math and science and working with incubators at Wright-Patterson Air Force Base.

Attrition is also a problem. Over one-third of the students who enroll leave before graduation, 17 percent of those for reasons beyond the school's control, including relocations. Some students fear that they will not be able to graduate within four years, and so they transfer to traditional schools. Some aren't physically up to the effort and time required because of family and other responsibilities. In the eight years of DECA's existence, however, there have been only four people who have dropped out of high school completely; students do go on to other schools, equipped with better tools for success than they arrived with.

Dave Taylor explains that since DECA is held to the same rules as other schools, failing students cannot be summarily dismissed:

> We are a charter school, and a charter school legally is a school district of one school, and no school district can deny a child an education, and so, in other words, if you are eligible to go to that school, I can't say to you, "You cannot go to this school." Once you've been admitted, you're allowed to stay, unless, of course, you're expelled, but even if you're expelled, you're allowed to return to the school. Expulsion only lasts thirty days. I can't just put you out. That's not a conversation that we have.
>
> What I do, I'll sit down with the parents and I'll show them the facts: here's where we are, here's where we're going, and I'm concerned about that. That's usually the conversation I have with the parents, but it's not acrimonious. It's not me getting up and grandstanding and saying, "Your child can't make it here," it's not that kind of conversation at all. It's generally: "Here are the options. Here's where we have progressed to from day one. If it were my child, here's what I would do, and therefore that is my recommendation to you. Here's what you can do. You can do that, or you can do this, this, and this, so what's the plan?"
>
> I find that the parents are responsive to that, because it's not being shoved down their throats, and they do realize that we genuinely care. It's never about money, for any of us. It's not about accolades. It's really about doing what's best for the child. I'll sit down with the kid, and I'll say, "I want you to finish here, but more importantly, I want you to finish, and you've got to graduate from high school, friend." That conversation is not fun, but it's important.

Because of the attrition, and because students come to DECA so far behind—coming into the junior high years with third-, fourth-, fifth-, or sixth-grade skills—DECA has established a K–12 DECA Prep School under the sponsorship of the Fordham Foundation.

"We can't run any faster," says Judy Hennessey. "We have extended the school day, we have extended it to Saturday for test prep, we have weekend review sessions, and we have about three-quarters of our student body involved in summer, so we just can't run any faster or put any more pressure on the high schoolers to be prepared, so I would say we have run out of time. We believe that the national research would say that if the student isn't reading on the third-grade level by third grade, the chances are you're not going to get them to college."

In the meantime, DECA will continue to contribute to the education community, as other charter schools have done. Steven Brill cites Jon Schnur and other reformers who "argue that the larger significance of charter schools is that the ones that work not only demonstrate that children from the most challenged homes and communities can learn but also support how traditional public schools might be changed to make them operate effectively."[7]

Can DECA's success be replicated at other schools? "Yes," Tom Lasley would reply:

> I think a lot of the things that DECA does are replicable. The focus on trying to identify and hire good teachers. Anybody can do that. The focus on trying to identify and hire a good principal. Anybody can do that. A focus on delivering a rigorous curriculum. The common core standards that forty-three states have now adopted, and Ohio is one of the adopting states—that's going to ramp up the rigor, the academic rigor in the curriculum. Anybody can do that. The strong advising system that DECA has—Judy and everybody else will tell you historically that's been one of their strengths. Anybody can do that.
>
> I think essentially almost everything that they're doing that makes them unique and strong is doable anyplace else. It may just look a little bit different somewhere else.

DECA senior Bryson adds his opinion: "I don't know if it will be on the same level. It's like they started from scratch and the whole experience is what makes DECA so great. If a school is modeled after us, they don't start where we did, where we didn't know what to do. It's like it's the whole experience and the whole journey that made DECA so great. I'm sure they'll be great too, but it's just on a different level."

We're asked this every week, dozens of times," Judy replies. "And my answer is a resounding 'yes.' This model is not person-specific or place-specific, and it doesn't have to be a pure replication. The fidelity to this model is not what's important, it's the tenets, like a personalized school environment, a faculty that is invested and has a lot of autonomy, the seeking out of corporate leaders to help guide a school district, the notion that parents have to be held accountable, as well as their children."

Dave Taylor's answer is a qualified "yes":

> At the Dayton Public Schools? No. That's obviously the short answer. The long answer to that is that there are a number of things that we do that could be replicated. I think that to say that DECA works for every kid is a huge, huge misstatement and not even remotely close to being true. The fact of the matter is that there are probably fifteen or twenty things that we do at our school that could be discussed with the district and could be assimilated.
>
> That's actually why we did our Institute this summer, where we went through them and we laid out what are some of the things that make us special and we began to disseminate them to other schools, because it's not about keeping secrets. It's really about how do we improve our learning pursuits. If we just had a school comment that we want to be like DECA and it was started and the city wanted to know if it would be successful. It might, it might not. I simply do not know, but you have to have a lot of the pieces in place in order to make that happen.
>
> I'm big on not being arrogant as a school, because we truly are blessed in a lot of ways, and I don't know if I were principal of Patterson-Kennedy or one

other of the Dayton public schools, that we would have the results that we do, because the bottom line is the discussion that we have is much different than the discussion that they're having at one of those schools.

In those schools they're serving all kids, kids who don't care about school, kids who want to be mechanics, kids who want to be doctors. For us, the argument stops with "You say you're going to college, so here's what you need to do to make that happen." And because not every student starts off with that mentality in mind, there is a difference there, and I'm not going to sit here and act like it's the same thing. It's not.

The DECA Institute was begun in the summer of 2011 as a response to this very question. With a dissemination grant from the Public Charter School Program, DECA hosted educators from all over Ohio for two days of "What do we do at DECA that can be replicated?" Almost all were urban educators who can continue communicating with one another through social web-based networking.

One DECA innovation that it shared with the educators is the Management Analysis Network, or "MAN," which, as the Institute handbook explains, "is a Student Information System created by DECA, Jobs for the Future, and SysInterface which enables teachers and staff to view and track data for students from grades 9–12. More than just a traditional gradebook, the MAN allows DECA's teachers to grade students based upon State and National Educational Standards, Benchmarks and Indicators," such as the nontraditional ones used by the school.

"The MAN also allows DECA's staff to track Standardized Test data, Gateway status, and College Classes, as well as Community Involvement. The MAN is an evolving tool as DECA is trying to expand the data tracking and reporting capability it provides."

Not only is MAN evolving, but the school itself continues to evolve as it seeks to avail itself of the latest technology. Tom Lasley predicts that in the not-too-distant future DECA will be looking at "virtual requirements." "What would happen if DECA said to its students, 'To graduate from DECA, you have to take at least one virtual course. You decide which one.'" Or it might decide to multiply the effectiveness of its teachers by using "blended learning," as some hybrid schools in California have done, combining computers with face-to-face instruction.

This is indeed what is envisaged in the future for the recently established K–12 DECA prep school, thus allowing individualized instruction for a heterogeneous mix of urban students while optimizing the use of precious staff talent.

In the tradition of continuing relationships with students and graduates, DECA's governing board is also establishing an organization to help its alumni find the appropriate jobs when they graduate from college, so that their education will be put to good use.

In spite of the bumps in the road it has encountered, DECA will continue to grow, improve, and make its mark on the community.

NOTES

1. Chester E. Finn Jr., Terry Ryan, and Michael B. Lafferty, *Ohio's Education Reform Challenges: Lessons from the Frontlines* (New York: Palgrave/Macmillan, 2010), 72.

2. Finn, Ryan, and Lafferty, *Ohio's Education Reform Challenges*, 72.

3. Steven Brill, *Class Warfare: Inside the Fight to Fix America's Schools* (New York: Simon & Schuster, 2011), 8.

4. Randy Tucker and Ken McCall, "Ohio Trails U.S. Average for Four-year Degrees," *Dayton Daily News*, September 22, 2011.

5. Abigail Thernstrom and Stephan Thernstrom, *No Excuses: Closing the Racial Gap in Learning* (New York: Simon & Schuster, 2003), 33.

6. Thernstrom and Thernstrom, *No Excuses*, 34.

7. Thernstrom and Thernstrom, *No Excuses*, 9.

Conclusion

Suppose we wanted to create the ideal school for inner-city children. Thomas Lasley has given much thought to what it takes. "There are certain things that good schools have in common," he says.

First, they really do have high-quality teachers. There's no doubt that the teacher is the most important dynamic, so, pretty consistently across the schools that I've seen that are performing well, you see very, very committed and high-quality teachers, so, yes, that would be the first thing.

I think they also have school leaders, principals, that all possess a pretty singular vision of where they want to go. Some of the less effective schools have managers that are able to administer all the different operations of the school, but they don't put a priority of one thing over another . . .

I think the schools where you find effective leaders are the ones where the principal is saying to him or herself, "Look, first and foremost, we're here to make sure our kids learn, and the good meals, the cleanliness in the school—all those things are important—but fundamentally, we're here to make sure that the kids learn."

In everything they do, they're always making certain that they're driving toward that goal, and I don't think it's at all unlike what you find in business or in corporate America. A good corporate leader says, "Here's exactly what we're trying to do, achieve it," and everything they do is directed toward that goal. Even though during the day they may have to do a, b, or c, they're still trying to accomplish it.

So if you have good teachers and if you have a good school leader, you probably are 80 percent of the way home in terms of having the school that you want.

And then, I'll list one more. Do they have a really sound curriculum? And a curriculum that is driving toward certain performance metrics. So, if I have good teachers, good administrator, and I've got pretty clear performance metrics, I'll bet on that school.

DECA would surely make the honor roll on all of the above.

* * *

Let's imagine a checklist of the factors that other top educators deem essential. How would DECA fare? It might look something like this:

CHECKLIST[1]

School Environment

- Safe
- Family like
- Access to mentors
- Everyone accountable
- Community ties
- Parents engaged

Classes

- Small size
- Students work in groups, collaborate

Learning

- Student centered, student directed
- Teacher–student teamwork, guided discovery
- Focus on character and discipline
- Innovative, creative, experiential, authentic
- Varied teaching methods
- Hands-on
- Includes "tool-kit" of skills, habits, styles
- Active and personalized
- Open to technical support
- Good assessment methods, frequent assessment to make adjustments, use of data to measure student performance and drive improvement
- Scaffolding to support student while learning

Principals

- Have authority
- Involved with and support teachers
- Not burdened by bureaucracy

- Have power and responsibility
- Principals free to hire and fire without union interference
- Have a vision, goals, plans
- Have freedom to shape curriculum

Teachers

- Dedicated
- High quality, well educated
- Focused, caring
- Respect students
- Free to teach, no administrative duties
- Plan well
- High expectations
- Culturally sensitive
- Free of stranglehold of bureaucratic, political, and union rules, have as much autonomy as possible
- Have power and responsibility
- Collaborate with one another and with administration
- Have mentors, receive collegial advice
- Act as role models, teach students there is more to life than present situation

Curriculum

- School has freedom to shape
- Challenging
- Offers broad education
- Based on goals

* * *

If we compare our checklists above to the sheet that a pilot verifies before he takes to the skies, then DECA is well prepared to soar into the heavens. It joins the ranks of other outstanding schools, like the KIPP schools, Harlem Success Academy, Newark's North Star Academy, and others that have followed similar pathways to success.

DECA's contributions do not end at the classroom doors, however, as students and graduates give back to the community. They bring to mind *The Hero with a Thousand Faces*, by Joseph Campbell, who wrote of one myth that exists in every culture, past, and present. [2]

According to his writings, the hero must venture forth from his familiar world, often having helpers who facilitate the journey. On the threshold of the adventure, the hero must suffer an ordeal of some sort, followed by further trials to be undergone in order to receive the benefits of the adventure. Having completed his mission, he returns home to share what he has gained with the community. It's easy to see many parallels to what DECA's young people experience, as DECA students look to use their education to improve the inner city.

Many of the students believe that they can counteract the despair of their community, giving its residents exposure to a better way of life. The cause of the inner city's problems, they claim, is that its inhabitants know no other world. They lack perspective, the students say. From Andre, who has many drug addicts in his family: "I know my cousins always said, 'I'm going to do what my brother did, I'm going to do what my uncle did, I'm going to do what my father did, because there's nothing out there left for us to do.'"

Damarion, too, would like to alleviate the despair of the inner city: "My best solution to the problem would be to just try to talk to these young men and just try to break into their minds, because I know that they have such a closed mindset on how things are. Just try to open up their minds about what's really out there in the world if they apply themselves and not just stay in the streets and do what they're doing now, because eventually it's going to get them killed or in jail."

Daron thinks "the major contributing factor" in the problems of the urban poor "is the lack of perspective and perception."

> It's often said that you're a product of your environment. A lot of people growing up in those kinds of neighborhoods tend to think, "Well, this is all I'm going to see. This is all I know, so I'm not going to walk onto unfamiliar ground." So I think it's more like not seeing the greater things in life, in real life. . . . When you don't have exposure, you don't know what's out there, and you don't know the possibilities, the infinite possibilities that exist. That's a major thing.
>
> It's like being in a dark hole and never seeing the light, or you see the light, but it's a little speck. You know it's there, but you've never tasted it, and you've never been there to experience it. . . . So it's mostly lack of exposure, lack of experience. Staying in the here and now.
>
> And it's sad, because when I'm on the bus I hear a lot of young people say, "Yeah, I'm going to have kids, and we're going to be on welfare," and I think to myself, "It's greater than that. There's more to life than just engaging in what you see and only accepting what you see as what life really is."

Recalling his athlete friends who would not leave home to seek a better life, Alonzo agrees that "exposure is the key to learning and growing as an individual." Now that he's a college student, he notes that "when you get to college you learn that the person that does the best is not necessarily the smartest. It's exposure, along with the work ethic, that lead to success." He adds:

I remember my sophomore year at DECA, Mr. Jones asked the class, "Do you think I'm smarter than you?" And we laughed. "Yeah, you've got this college degree in biology and all that." And he was like, "I'm not smarter than you. It's just the fact that I've just been exposed to more than you have." And when he said that, I looked at it that way.

Now when I talk to people I'm really able to see that exposure really makes you smarter, more intelligent, because the more exposure you have, it broadens your horizon, gives you more things to discuss. You're adaptable to more things—you're adaptable to more things, and you know more things.

The DECA students like to think of themselves as role models for those who have lacked exposure. As Jolena says, when people see the positive results of their education, they think, "'Well, maybe they're doing something right.' I think it all has to do with the results. If you couldn't see the results, it would still be a positive, but they obviously see how beneficial this is to us."

To help the inner city, she would start with "making everyone aware of issues, major issues, that affect everyday life, everyone's life. I think it comes from people not knowing exactly what to do, so I think we would have more recreation centers, more guided time with the young, and things of that sort, so that they learn at a young age the right way and the wrong way, and people who guide them and motivate them going toward the right path, instead of the wrong. . . . It's a job for women, as well as men, because their nurturing side makes them want to help everyone, not just themselves."

She would like to make people aware that there is help, if they would only seek it.

"Seeing the statistics," Bryson says,

it looks like the neighborhoods are just horrible places. But it's not that all the time. We do a lot of things—like in the area I live in, they do a lot of community things.

A lot of the churches are in there trying to do something and to help out, and so it's not so horrible as sometimes particularly the news makes it seem, but it's not where it could be . . . [Those in the inner-city need] better role models and people willing to go out to these neighborhoods, and to pick them up and to encourage them. We need those adults, those people, who can connect with the people in those neighborhoods to come and to work to actually help them so they see that there are people out there willing.

There are indeed groups like a church-sponsored organization called "The Victory Project," begun by a former police officer, that seeks to mentor young people who have been through the juvenile justice system. Churches have helped young men like Andre, whose pastor has been an important influence on him. Alonzo's church has been a big part of his life, but, he says, they could be doing much more.

Andre makes the point, however, that it's up the people who need help to come to the churches and ask for mentoring from church members or from the pastors themselves. It's a difficult decision to make when you know no other way.

Kaneesha has turned her negative background into a positive for the community. The child who had been shuffled from one foster home to another was recently adopted by her latest foster family. Now she's serving on the Children's Services Youth Advisory Board. The organization's first president and vice president were DECA students when the group was begun some six years ago. She describes what it does:

> We have meetings about issues with the foster-care system. Recently we went to Washington, D.C., to talk to congressmen about some issues about the youth in foster care, how some of them are not being able to make it to school, because the foster parents will not give them bus fare, and some of their documents can be missing so when they fill out school paperwork, the school cannot provide them with bus passes, like normal school, because some of the information is missing.
>
> So we went down there to talk to them about that, we went down there to speak to them on creating better foster-care training, training for the foster parents, because sometimes there'll be certain situations where the foster parent does not know how to handle it. We decided that they should have better foster-parent training to come from all directions, so if something is thrown at the foster parents, they know how to approach it better.
>
> And I'm part of FCAA, Foster Care Alumni of America. We meet up sometimes in Cincinnati, sometimes in Columbus, and the Youth Advisory Board goes to those meetings so we can train Youth Advisory Boards. We just helped them set up a Youth Advisory Board in Cincinnati.

She's also on the board of FLOC, "For the Love of Children":

> We create activities for the children in the communities to do. For example, some students want to go to the prom, but they can't afford tuxedos and dresses. We have organizations where people donate their dresses and their tuxes and then the child can come in and look through dresses and we help them find a dress that they like the best. They get the dress and the tux at no cost. With FLOC we help them pick out dresses for the Winter Ball. And during Christmas we do the toy drive, where families come in and we give them presents for their child, and the child can work through and pick out gifts on their own.

As Bryson says, "We're not just doing this for ourselves, we want to do this for our families, for everybody. I mention young males specifically because we don't have a lot geared toward helping them to mature and to show them that somebody really cares about them, because I've found that a lot of times they feel as though they have no inspiration, they don't have anyone rallying on their behalf. I want to just give them some type of role model. I'm close to their age, but they see me trying to do something different."

Jewel, who encouraged her cousin Alonzo to attend DECA, wants to inspire other family members as well. "In my family, some people didn't even graduate from high school, and none ever really completed college or even attended college, and so I feel a need to raise the bar for my family. If I can do it, I feel like they can do it, and so that little kid in me wants to keep on dreaming and keep on raising the bar. That's what I try to keep on doing every day."

Virtually all the students plan to return to help in their old neighborhoods after college. LaTonya, the future lawyer, sees so much that could be done in her hometown:

> I do eventually want to come back to Dayton and give back to Dayton, because there are a lot of things that need to be rebuilt, I feel. There are a lot of buildings that need to be rebuilt, abandoned houses that need to be torn down or rebuilt, because there are a lot of homeless people, so give them housing, as well as mentoring young men, as well as young women. It's just something I want to do.

"I want to come back," Andre says. "I would come back to visit high schools and talk to them about success and how I made a success, and how I changed, because my lifestyle had been bad."

Bryson, who looks to a teaching career, "definitely" will return home. "If I can't teach at DECA," his first choice, "I'll be somewhere in Dayton, teaching language arts or math."

"I honestly feel obligated to really come back and do something for my community," says Vanetta, now in college.

> I want to do like a nonprofit. I might want to come back and start my own nonprofit, something here or work with another group. I like cars, and I even thought about something like if I had a shop here, even filtering in students from the automotive programs, like an apprentice program to allow them to gain more skills and get some form of employment. So I really want to do something.
>
> I see Dayton falling behind, falling back, but I would love to see the economy come back and people give back and we would just bring you back up. I would love to be a part of that.

Alonzo, a senior in college, makes it a point to visit high schools when he's back in town. "I'll go to a lot of different schools and maybe e-mail the principal and see if there are any students they want me to talk to. At Thurgood Marshall High School, I've spoken specifically to fifteen students, and in the summer I actually had my own kind of mini-session, as to the steps that you need to take in order to go to college, with parents and students, so in the room at a time there could be anywhere from twenty to thirty people."

What would Alonzo do to change the problems of the city? He says, with a laugh,

> Well, I always joke around—well, I joke in a sense, but I'm kind of serious. I say I'll come back and be mayor, and some of the other males that graduated from DECA, I'll put them in certain positions and offices and we will turn the city around.
>
> Educationally, my ultimate plan is I want to become a teacher, but I want to open up my own school where I have my own curriculum, because when I went to Senegal [last summer], I noticed that those young people who were privileged enough to go to school, they actually saw calculus and physics in middle school. So my plan was to have a school, have my own curriculum and expose kids to calculus and physics and everything in preschool, because it's not the fact that we can't learn or we're not capable of learning, it's the fact that we don't get the exposure to it.
>
> I remember Mr. Jones telling me he had asked the students when they see calculus, and a lot of times they don't see calculus until they are seniors or they're freshmen in college, whereas in other countries, they may see calculus in middle school or freshman year.
>
> The fact that they have that prior exposure puts them in a better circumstance so that even if they didn't understand it the first time, from the fact that they saw it, they'll be more likely to understand it the second time. And so my main objective is to have a curriculum where I can expose children to the material that it seems like they don't get exposed to.

When we look at DECA's young people who have left their familiar world for the adventure and trials of a challenging education—and the rewards they return to share—it's not too much of a stretch to say they are heroes, all. And the greatest boon they bestow upon a despairing community is hope.

NOTES

1. A list of sources from which this checklist is compiled is furnished at the end of the References section.

2. Joseph Campbell, *The Hero with a Thousand Faces* (Princeton: Princeton University Press, 1949).

References

Alexander, Michelle. *The New Jim Crow: Mass Incarceration in the Age of Colorblindness.* New York: The New Press, 2010.

Allen, Colin. "Absentee Fathers and Teen Pregnancy." *Psychology Today*, May 1, 2003.

Anderson, Elijah. *Code of the Street: Decency, Violence, and the Moral Life of the Inner City.* New York: Norton, 1999.

Battelle for Kids. *Global Education Study.* 2012.

Bennish, Steve. "Tax Incentives May Spur Local Factories." *Dayton Daily News*, January 26, 2012.

Bennish, Steve, Kelli Wynn, and Doug Page. "One Local Gang Maintains Power, Influence in City." *Dayton Daily News*, March 10, 2012.

Bremner, J. Douglas. "The Lasting Effects of Psychological Trauma on Memory and the Hippocampus." www.lawandpsychiatry.com/html/hippocampus.htm.

Brill, Steven. *Class Warfare: Inside the Fight to Fix America's Schools.* New York: Simon & Schuster, 2011.

Brown, Tony. *Black Lies, White Lies.* New York: Morrow, 1995.

Buck, Stuart. *Acting White: The Ironic Legacy of Desegregation.* New Haven, CT: Yale University Press, 2010.

Campbell, Joseph, *The Hero with a Thousand Faces* (Princeton: Princeton University Press, 1949).

Canada, Geoffrey. "Bringing Change to Scale: The Next Big Reform Challenge." In Karl Weber, ed., *Waiting for "Superman": How We Can Save America's Failing Public Schools* , 189–200. New York: Public Affairs, 2010.

———. *Fist, Stick, Knife, Gun: A Personal Story of Violence.* Boston: Beacon Press, 1995; rev. ed. 2010.

———. *Reaching up for Manhood: Transforming the Lives of Boys in America.* Boston: Beacon Press, 1998.

Carlson Robert G., and Harvey A. Siegal. "The Crack Life: An Ethnographic Overview of Crack Use and Sexual Behavior among African-Americans in a Midwest Metropolitan City." *Journal of Psychoactive Drugs* 23, no. 1 (January–March 1991): 12.

Carter, Samuel Casey. *On Purpose: How Great School Cultures Form Character.* Thousand Oaks, CA: Corwin/Sage, 2011.

Christie, Ron. *Acting White: The Curious History of a Racial Slur.* New York: Thomas Dunn/ St. Martin's Press, 2010.

College Board Advocacy and Policy Center and the Business Innovation Factory. *The Educational Experience of Young Men of Color: Capturing the Student Voice.* September 2010.

Common Core State Standards Initiative. www.corestandards.org/the-standards.

Cookson, Peter W., Jr., and Kristina Berger. *Expect Miracles: Charter Schools and the Politics of Hope and Despair.* Boulder, CO: Westview Press, 2002.

Corwin, Miles. *And Still We Rise: The Trials and Triumphs of Twelve Gifted Inner-City Students.* New York: HarperCollins, 2000.

Cosby, William H., Jr., and Alvin F. Poussaint. *Come On, People.* Nashville: Thomas Nelson, 2007.

"Dayton Crime Rate Report (Ohio)." www.cityrating.com/crime-statistics/ohio/dayton.html.

Dayton Daily News, "Drug Czar Unveils Plan to Attack Medication Abuse," April 20, 2011.

———. "Retaliation Shootings Put Children in Danger," April 19, 2011.

———. "Suspects Sought in Shooting of 2 Children," April 16, 2011.

Delpit, Lisa. *Other People's Children: Cultural Conflict in the Classroom.* New York: The New Press, 2006.

Deneen, James, and Carm Catanese. *Urban Schools: Crisis and Revolution.* Lanham, MD: Rowman & Littlefield, 2011.

Early College High School Initiative. "Overview FAQ." www.earlycolleges.org/overview.html.

Finn, Chester E., Jr., Terry Ryan, and Michael B. Lafferty. *Ohio's Education Reform Challenges: Lessons from the Frontlines.* New York: Palgrave/Macmillan, 2010.

Foster, Karen C., and Michael Nakkula. *Early College High School: Igniting and Sustaining Educational Identity Development.* Harvard Graduate School of Education Risk and Prevention Program. December 7, 2004.

Friedman, Thomas L. "My Little (Global) School." *New York Times*, April 3, 2013.

Frolik, Cornelius. "Jobless Rate for Single Moms at 25-Year High." *Dayton Daily News*, November 12, 2011.

Giardino, Angelo P., Tol Blakeley Harris, and Eileen E. Giardino. "Child Abuse and Neglect, Posttraumatic Stress Disorder." July 28, 2009.

Ginsberg, Alice E. *Embracing Risk in Urban Education.* Lanham, MD: Rowman & Littlefield Education, 2012.

Gokavi, Mark. "Students Getting Free Lunches at School Kept Anonymous." *Dayton Daily News*, March 4, 2010.

Good, Thomas L., and Jere E. Brophy. *Looking in Classrooms*, 8th ed. New York: Addison-Wesley, 2000.

Goodnough, Abby, and Katie Zezima. "Newly Born, and Withdrawing from Painkillers." *New York Times*, April 10, 2011.

Hall, Edward T. *Beyond Culture.* New York: Anchor, 1989. First published 1976.

Hanushek, Eric. "The Difference Is Great Teachers." In Karl Weber, ed., *Waiting for "Superman": How We Can Save America's Failing Public Schools*, 81–100. New York: Public Affairs, 2010.

Harvard Graduate School of Education. "Technical Working Report." December 2004.

Harvard Graduate School of Education/Jobs for the Future. "Early College High School Study." June 18, 2004.

———. "Preliminary Quantitative Findings." December 2004.

Hettleman, Kalman R. *It's the Classroom, Stupid: A Plan to Save America's Schoolchildren.* Lanham, MD: Rowman & Littlefield Education, 2010.

"How TV Affects Your Child." KidsHealth. www.kidshealth.org/parent/positive/family/tv_affects_child.html.

Huesmann, L. Rowell, Jessica Moise-Titus, Cheryl-Lynn Podolski, and Leonard D. Eron. "Longitudinal Relations between Children's Exposure to TV Violence and Their Aggressive and Violent Behavior in Young Adulthood: 1977–1992." *Development Psychology* 39, no. 2 (2003).

Institute on Domestic Violence in the African American Community. www. Dvinstitute.org.

Jones, Jacqueline. *Labor of Love, Labor of Sorrow: Black Women, Work, and the Family, from Slavery to the Present*, rev. ed. New York: Basic Books, 2010.

Katsuyama, R. M. "Character Education in Ohio Schools: Results of the Partners in Character Evaluation Study, 1998–2002." 2004. Ohio Partners in Character Education. October 21, 2010. www.charactereducationohio.org/utilities/evaluationsummary5-06.pdf.

Kinchelow, Joe L., kecia hayes, Karel Rose, and Philip M. Anderson, eds. and introduction, *Urban Education: A Comprehensive Guide for Educators, Parents, and Teachers.* Lanham, MD: Rowman & Littlefield Education, 2007.

Kitwana, Bakari. *The Hip-Hop Generation: Young Blacks and the Crisis in African-American Culture.* New York: Basic Books, 2002.

Kopp, Wendy. *One Day, All Children: The Unlikely Triumph of Teach for America and What I Learned Along the Way.* New York: Public Affairs/Perseus Book Group, 2001.

Kopp, Wendy, and Steven Farr. *A Chance to Make History: What Works and What Doesn't in Providing an Excellent Education for All.* New York: Public Affairs/Perseus, 2011.

Kozol, Jonathan. *Amazing Grace: The Lives of Children and the Conscience of a Nation.* New York: HarperCollins, 1995.

———. *The Shame of the Nation: The Restoration of Apartheid Schooling in America.* New York: Three Rivers Press, 2005.

Kuyk, Betty. *African Voices in the African American Heritage.* Bloomington: Indiana University Press, 2003.

Ladson-Billings, Gloria. *The Dream-Keepers: Successful Teachers of African American Children,* 2nd ed. San Francisco: Jossey-Bass/Wiley, 2009.

Landsman, Julie. *A White Teacher Talks about Race.* Lanham, MD: Scarecrow Press, 2001.

Lang, Susan L., "Most teens get pregnant on purpose because other life goals seem out of reach, says Cornell researcher," *Cornell Chronicle,* June, 1997.

Lasley, Thomas J. II, Thomas J. Matczynski, and James B. Rowley. *Instructional Models: Strategies for Teaching in a Diverse Society,* 2nd ed. Belmont, CA: Wadsworth/Thomson Learning. 2002.

Lindsley, Evangeline, and Nancy Brown Diggs. *My Century: An Outspoken Memoir.* Dayton, OH: Landfall Press, 1997.

Los Angeles Times. "Drug Deaths Now Outnumber Traffic Fatalities in U.S., Data Show," September 17, 2011. www.articles.latimes/com/2011/sep/17/local/la-me-drugs-epidemic-20110918.

Lynn, Marvin, A. Dee Williams, Grace Benigno, Colleen Mitchell, and Gloria Park. "Race, Class, and Gender in Urban Education: Exploring the Critical Research on Urban Pedagogy and School Reform." In Joe L. Kincheloe, kecia hayes, Karel Rose, and Philip M. Anderson, eds., *Urban Education: A Comprehensive Guide for Educators, Parents, and Teachers,* 89–101. Lanham, MD: Rowman & Littlefield Education, 2007.

Mazza, James J., and William M. Reynolds, "Exposure to Violence in Young Inner-City Adolescents: Relationships with Suicidal Ideation, Depression, and PTSD Symptomatology." *Journal of Abnormal Child Psychology* 27, no. 3 (1999): 203–13.

McWhorter, John. *Winning the Race: Beyond the Crisis in Black America.* New York: Gotham/Penguin, 2006.

Meyer, Peter. *Needles in a Haystack: Lessons from Ohio's High-Performing Urban High Schools.* Washington, DC: Fordham Institute, 2012.

Moore, Wes. *The Other Wes Moore: One Name, Two Fates.* New York: Spiegel and Grau, 2010.

Nakkula, Michael, and Marie Onaga. "Transitioning to College: Year Four of the E.C.H.S. Study." Boston: Jobs for the Future and Harvard Graduate School of Education. May 7, 2008.

Oliver, William. *The Violent Social World of Black Men.* New York: Wiley/Jossey-Bass, 2001.

Ornstein, Allan C., and Thomas J. Lasley II. *Strategies for Effective Teaching,* 4th ed. Boston: McGraw Hill, 2004.

Paige, Rod, and Elaine Witty. *The Black-White Achievement Gap: Why Closing It Is the Greatest Civil Rights Issue of Our Time.* New York: American Management Association, 2010.

Patterson, James T. *Freedom Is Not Enough.* New York: Basic Books, 2010.

Paul, Annie Murphy. "School of Hard Knocks." Review of *How Children Succeed,* by Paul Tough. *New York Times,* August 23, 2012.

Payne, Ruby K. *A Framework for Understanding Poverty,* 4th rev. ed. Highlands, TX: AHA! Process, Inc., 2005.

Ravitch, Diane. *The Death and Life of the Great American School System: How Testing and Choice Are Undermining Education.* New York: Basic Books, 2010.

Rich, John A. *Wrong Place, Wrong Time.* Baltimore, MD: Johns Hopkins University Press, 2009.

Rowell, James D. "Kids' Needs and the Attention of Gangs," *Police Magazine*, June 1, 2000.

Samovar, Larry A., Richard E. Porter, and Edwin R. McDaniel. *Communication between Cultures*, 7th ed. Belmont, CA: Thomson/Wadsworth, 2010.

Sampson, William A. *Black Student Achievement.* Lanham, MD: Rowman & Littlefield Education, 2002.

Schubiner, Howard, Richard Scott, and Angela Tzelepis. "Exposure to Violence among Inner-city Youth." *Journal of Adolescent Health* 14, no. 3 (1992): 214–19. www.ncbi.nlm.nih/gov/pubmed/8323933.

Shipler, David K. *A Country of Strangers: Blacks and Whites in America.* New York: Knopf, 1997.

Smarick, Andy. *The Urban School System of the Future: Applying the Principles and Lessons of Chartering.* Lanham, MD: Rowman & Littlefield Education, 2012.

Sowell, Thomas. *Black Rednecks and White Liberals.* San Francisco: Encounter Books, 2005.

Strickland, Bill. "How Schools Kill Neighborhoods—And Can Help Save Them." In Karl Weber, ed., *Waiting for "Superman": How We Can Save America's Failing Public Schools*, 69–80. New York: Public Affairs, 2010.

Sum, Andrew, Ishwar Khatiwada, Joseph McLaughlin, and Paulo Tobar. *The Educational Attainment of the Nation's Young Black Men and Their Recent Labor Market Experiences: What Can Be Done to Improve Their Future Labor Market and Educational Prospects?* Boston: Center for Labor Market Studies, Northeastern University, 2007.

Sutherly, Ben. "Local Accidental Drug Overdose Deaths Twice as Much as Similar Ohio Counties," *Dayton Daily News*, January 27, 2011.

Tavernise, Sabrina. "Ohio County Losing Its Young to Painkillers' Grip." *New York Times*, April 20, 2011.

Thernstrom, Abigail, and Stephan Thernstrom. *No Excuses: Closing the Racial Gap.* New York: Simon & Schuster, 2003.

Tough, Paul. *How Children Succeed: Grit, Curiosity, and the Hidden Power of Character.* New York: Houghton Mifflin Harcourt, 2012.

———. *Whatever It Takes: Geoffrey Canada's Quest to Change Harlem and America.* Boston: Mariner/Houghton Mifflin Harcourt, 2008.

Tucker, Randy, and Ken McCall. "Ohio Trails U.S. Average for Four-year Degrees." *Dayton Daily News*, September 22, 2011.

U.S. Department of Veterans Affairs. "Effects of Community Violence on Children and Teens." National Center for PTSD. www.ptsd.va.gov/public/pages/effects-community-violence-children.asp.

Weber, Karl, ed. and introduction. *Waiting for "Superman": How We Can Save America's Failing Public Schools.* New York: Public Affairs, 2010.

West, Cornel. *Race Matters.* Boston: Beacon Press, 1993.

Whitman, David. *Sweating the Small Stuff: Inner-City Schools and the New Paternalism.* Washington, DC: Fordham Institute, 2008.

Williams, Andrew. *Working with Street Children.* Lyme Regis, UK: Russell House Publishing Ltd., 2011.

Williams, Juan. *Enough: The Phony Leaders, Dead End Movements, and Culture of Failure That Are Undermining Black America—And What We Can Do About It.* New York: Three Rivers Press, 2006.

Zemelman, Steven, Harvey Daniels, and Arthur Hyde. *Best Practice: Today's Standards for Teaching and Learning in America's Schools.* Portsmouth, NH: Heinemann, 2005.

CHECKLIST SOURCES

Battelle for Kids. *Global Education Study.* 2012.

Canada, Geoffrey. *Fist, Stick, Knife, Gun: A Personal Story of Violence.* Boston: Beacon Press, 1995.

Carter, Samuel Casey. *On Purpose: How Great School Cultures Form Character.* Thousand Oaks, CA: Corwin/Sage, 2011.

Corwin, Miles. *And Still We Rise: The Trials and Triumphs of Twelve Gifted Inner-City Students.* New York: HarperCollins, 2000.

Delpit, Lisa. *Other People's Children: Cultural Conflict in the Classroom.* New York: The New Press, 2006.

Deneen, James, and Carm Catanese. *Urban Schools: Crisis and Revolution.* Lanham, MD: Rowman & Littlefield, 2011.

Finn, Chester E., Jr., Terry Ryan, and Michael B. Lafferty. *Ohio's Education Reform Challenges: Lessons from the Frontlines.* New York: Palgrave/Macmillan, 2010.

Foster, Karen C., and Michael Nakkula, *Early College High School: Igniting and Sustaining Educational Identity Development.* Harvard Graduate School of Education Risk and Prevention Program, December 7, 2004.

Ginsberg, Alice E. *Embracing Risk in Urban Education.* Lanham, MD: Rowman & Littlefield Education, 2012.

Good, Thomas L., and Jere E. Brophy. *Looking in Classrooms*, 8th ed. New York: Addison-Wesley, 2000.

Hall, Edward T. *Beyond Culture.* New York: Anchor, 1989. First published 1976.

Harvard Graduate School of Education. "Technical Working Report." December 2004.

Hettleman, Kalman R. *It's the Classroom, Stupid: A Plan to Save America's Schoolchildren.* Lanham, MD: Rowman & Littlefield Education, 2010.

Kincheloe, Joe L., kecia hayes, Karel Rose, and Philip M. Anderson, eds. and introduction. *Urban Education: A Comprehensive Guide for Educators, Parents, and Teachers.* Lanham, MD: Rowman & Littlefield Education, 2007.

Kopp, Wendy. *One Day, All Children: The Unlikely Triumph of Teach for America and What I Learned Along the Way.* New York: Public Affairs/Perseus Book Group, 2001.

Kopp, Wendy, and Steven Farr. *A Chance to Make History: What Works and What Doesn't in Providing an Excellent Education for All.* New York: Public Affairs/Perseus, 2011.

Ladson-Billings, Gloria. *The Dream-Keepers: Successful Teachers of African American Children*, 2nd ed. San Francisco: Jossey-Bass/Wiley, 2009.

Lasley, Thomas J., II, Thomas J. Matczynski, and James B. Rowley. *Instructional Models: Strategies for Teaching in a Diverse Society*, 2nd ed. Belmont, CA: Wadsworth/Thomson Learning. 2002.

Meyer, Peter. *Needles in a Haystack: Lessons from Ohio's High-Performing Urban High Schools.* Washington, DC: Fordham Institute, 2012.

Nakkula, Michael, and Marie Onaga, "Transitioning to College: Year Four of the E.C.H.S. Study." Boston: Jobs for the Future and Harvard Graduate School of Education. May 7, 2008.

Ornstein, Allan C., and Thomas J. Lasley II. *Strategies for Effective Teaching*, 4th ed. Boston: McGraw Hill, 2004.

Ravitch, Diane. *The Death and Life of the Great American School System: How Testing and Choice Are Undermining Education.* New York: Basic Books, 2010.

Thernstrom, Abigail, and Stephan Thernstrom. *No Excuses: Closing the Racial Gap in Learning.* New York: Simon & Schuster, 2003.

Tough, Paul. *How Children Succeed: Grit, Curiosity, and the Hidden Power of Character.* New York: Houghton Mifflin Harcourt, 2012.

———. *Whatever It Takes: Geoffrey Canada's Quest to Change Harlem and America.* Boston: Mariner/Houghton Mifflin Harcourt, 2008.

Weber, Karl, ed. and introduction. *Waiting for "Superman": How We Can Save America's Failing Public Schools.* New York: Public Affairs, 2010.

Whitman, David. *Sweating the Small Stuff: Inner-City Schools and the New Paternalism.* Washington, DC: Fordham Institute, 2008.

Zemelman, Steven, Harvey Daniels, and Arthur Hyde. *Best Practice: Today's Standards for Teaching and Learning in America's Schools.* Portsmouth, NH: Heinemann, 2005.

Index

About the Author

Nancy Brown Diggs's long interest in other cultures is reflected by her PhD in East Asian studies, as well as her fluency in French, Spanish, and German. She is the author of *Hidden in the Heartland: The New Wave of Immigrants and the Challenge to America*; *Looking Beyond the Mask: When American Women Marry Japanese Men*; and *Steel Butterflies: Japanese Women and the American Experience*, as well as coauthor of *A Look at Life in Northern Ireland*. With *Breaking the Cycle* she explores a culture closer to home, that of inner-city teens, and describes how, with the help of good schools, they, too, can achieve the American dream.